GAY AND LESBIAN *Weddings*

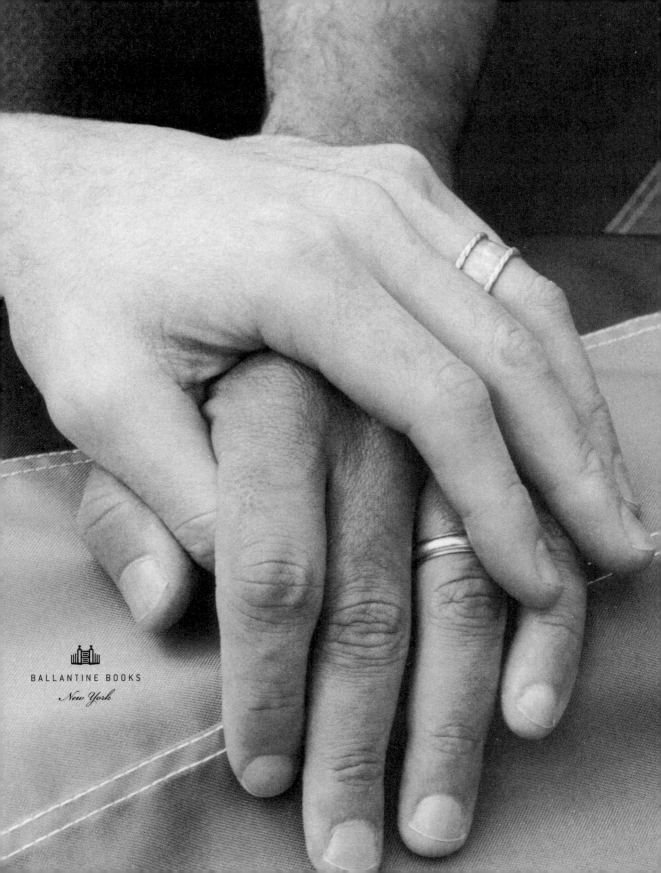

BALLANTINE BOOKS
New York

GAY AND LESBIAN *Weddings*

PLANNING THE PERFECT SAME–SEX CEREMONY

David Toussaint

with Heather Leo

*This book is dedicated to every gay and lesbian couple—past, present, and future—
who make the decision to say "I do." It is your commitment and determination—
and that beautiful four-letter word* love—*that have brought these pages to life.
While we may have put it together, you've done all the work.
For that you have our eternal gratitude.*

A Ballantine Book
Published by The Random House Publishing Group
Copyright © 2004 by David Toussaint
Photographs © 2004 by Piero Ribelli

All rights reserved under International and Pan-American
Copyright Conventions. Published in the United States by
Ballantine Books, an imprint of The Random House
Publishing Group, a division of Random House, Inc., New York,
and simultaneously in Canada by Random House
of Canada Limited, Toronto.

Ballantine and colophon are registered
trademarks of Random House, Inc.

www.ballantinebooks.com

ISBN 0-345-47574-7

Manufactured in the United States of America

987654321

FIRST EDITION

Book design by Casey Hampton

CONTENTS

4. *The Style Council*   59

Consider the pros and cons of the small, medium, and large wedding; choose a church or a beach wedding; and assess whether you are a casual or a formal type. Here are the specific questions to ask about your reception site to ensure your wishes are accommodated, a "Find Your Wedding Style" quiz, and a checklist of what to consider when planning the style of your ceremony and reception.

5. *The Wedding Party*   85

Choosing attendants, delegating tasks, and deciding whether to follow well-known wedding customs or create new ones are all important matters. Traditional etiquette and rituals such as throwing bouquets, entertaining bachelor/ette parties, purchasing engagement rings, and making up the guest list are covered here. Ideas for handling homophobia and giving straight answers to gay-wedding questions conclude the chapter.

6. *The 12-Step Wedding Planner*   109

A checklist for each step helps organize and simplify your planning.

7. *Creative Wedding Ideas*   183

This chapter provides alternative wedding ideas, including The Long Weekend, The Long Distance, The Surprise, and Theme Weddings. Personalize your ceremony, add cultural touches, and heed some definite "I don'ts."

8. *Sex-Rated*   193

Now that you're married, will your sex life change—or, more important, will it stay the same? If you haven't discussed your views on monogamy, now is a good time to do it. In this chapter, you'll find solutions to potential sex-busters such as body issues, long work nights, encroaching exes, flirting spouses, and family interference. You'll also find advice on keeping the spice in your marriage.

9. *Heavenly Honeymoons*   205

Did you know that resorts all over the world want *YOU*? Get the basics on preparing documents for travel abroad, packing right, securing suites for the sweeties, ensuring safety, and getting the royal treatment you deserve. Need help deciding whether to go traditional or all-gay? This chapter will break it down and help you follow your bliss.

GAY AND LESBIAN Weddings

IN THE
BEGINNING

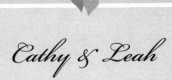

Cathy & Leah

WHO: Cathy Renna, thirty-eight, and Leah McElrath, thirty-nine.

WHEN: Saturday, November 22, 2003.

WHERE: Seaman's Church Institute, New York City. Eighty guests for a sunset family-style dinner at the institute. A southern–Italian combination of steak, chicken, and pasta platters.

THE SOUND OF MUSIC: Pop singer Randi Driscoll performed. "She's a little like Sarah McLachlan, but not as depressing," says Cathy.

THE SOUND OF SILENCE: No DJ. "We didn't want someone announcing the couple," says Cathy.

FIRST DANCE: "You Are So Beautiful."

THE WAY THEY WORE: Leah wore a custom-made cream-colored dress, which Cathy didn't see until the day of the wedding. Cathy wore a cream-colored tux jacket with black slacks.

IN ATTENDANCE: Cathy's sister and Leah's stepfather did readings.

NOTICEABLY ABSENT: Maids of honor, bridesmaids, flower girl, ushers.

HOLY MATRIMONY: The officiant is an elder with the Church of Christ in Washington, as well as an ordained Southern Baptist minister.

HOLY SURPRISE! He's also gay.

WHAT THEY OVERCAME: Convincing Cathy's mother it was a real wedding. "As much as she loves Leah, when it came to a wedding she had to gradually accept it. Once she got involved with the planning, she started to come around. Then she turned into the typical Long Island Italian mother and wondered if we paid the caterer in cash, if we'd get a discount."

AFTERGLOW: A simple Sunday brunch with close friends.

HONEYMOON G-SPOT: Two weeks at a beach house in Provincetown, dog in tow.

PARTING WORDS: "The wedding wasn't political," Cathy says. "It was along the lines of Quaker thinking, the idea that you ask for support from your community."

*C*hances are, there will be many different kinds of people picking up this book. Some of you will have, no doubt, already found the love of your life, and have just decided to cement your relationship with a gay wedding ceremony. Others will be somewhere in the midst of planning when you come to the realization that you need a little help along the way. There might even be dreamers among you, those of you who have either recently come out or are still struggling with your sexual identity, but know that a "marriage," legal or otherwise, is part of your life plan, like a house in the suburbs, two children, and a dog. Among you there might even be a parent, brother, or best friend of a gay man or woman who hopes that this book will make an honest, committed partner out of your gay or lesbian loved one. Finally, this book is for all of you, with love at heart and an open mind.

In a world that is not always so kind, we want to create something that is, above all, honest and positive. It's our goal to help you through the stages of what will, undoubtedly, be one of the most memorable times of your life. As you follow your heart on the way to wedded bliss, you'll be spreading positive energy throughout the world. Embrace yourselves, embrace your love, and enjoy the ride.

Let's get something, um, straight, right away. We're not going to tell you that relationships are perfect, or that getting married means you're headed for utopia. Which means, for starters, that we're assuming those of you planning a wedding have already slept with your partners. If you haven't, for God's sake put this book down and get to it. Just like you don't buy the car before taking it on a test drive, you never say "I do" until you can say "We've done it." And even if your union brings you memories to last a lifetime, that doesn't necessarily mean you'll spend the rest of your lives together. Sadly, 50 percent of heterosexual marriages end in divorce, and there's no indication that this statistic is going to change anytime soon. There's also no magical statistic we can give you to reassure you that the percentages will be any different for homosexual unions. And though much progress has been made in the past few decades—progress that needs to be celebrated and cherished every day—you'd be unwise to believe that, by having a wedding, homophobia will erase itself from the world, that those friends and relatives who haven't spoken to you since you announced you were gay will finally come around, or that you'll never again be discriminated against, be called a dirty name, or deal with any of the myriad other obstacles homosexuals face.

The good news is that, since you've made this decision knowing all of the above—it's highly unlikely you've decided to merge your lives because one of you is "in trouble"—you're making this decision because you're in love and truly do want to spend the rest of your lives together. This is not only the strongest argument for the support of legalized same-sex marriage, it's also the biggest reason why you should feel proud about planning a ceremony with friends and relatives. In one of the twenty-first century's first phenomena, gay men and women are becoming the New Romantics, the true pioneers in the next generation of married life.

So, Why a Wedding in the First Place?

Yes, you're in love, but why should that encourage you to celebrate with a wedding? Same-sex marriage is not legally recognized in the United States, and you probably already live with your partner. Assuming you invite more than two people to the ceremony, and serve something other than pigs-in-a-blanket and beer, you're going to be spending a lot of money on this event. You're also going to have to deal with most of the headaches that "real" marriage planning involves. Besides, it's not as if Tiffany will lock you out unless you sport wedding bands, or Sandals is on the verge of allowing same-sex couples to honeymoon at its Caribbean resorts. Finally, why on earth would you want to join a club that has, since the beginning of time, refused to have you as a member?

At first glance, it looks as if you're getting none of the perks and all of the pain. Yet judging by the numbers of same-sex ceremony notices in newspapers these days, the commitment ceremonies that have been recorded since Vermont passed a civil-union bill in 2000, and the remarkable dash-to-the-courthouse elopements in San Francisco, a heck of a lot of you want to get hitched.

The answers are more conventional than stereotypical views of gays and lesbians would lead you to believe.

Of all the couples we interviewed for this book, there were two answers to the question "Why a wedding?" that sprang up most consistently. The first was that a ceremony affirmed the relationship to family and friends; you were publicly identified as life partners who would be there for each other in sickness and health. We heard reports from couples that, after their ceremony, their immediate families started treating their unions as "marriages," by, for example, including partners in holidays and other major events they might not otherwise have been invited to. Some couples told us that their spouses were now asked to attend office parties and company picnics. There were even stories of no longer dealing with annoying "water cooler" chatter like, "So when are you going to finally settle down?" (even though the ones they were "settled down with" were already known to everyone at the office). Marriage ceremonies, legal or otherwise, legitimize relationships in the eyes of those whom many believe are the most important critics of all: friends and family.

The second answer that came up most was children. Gay men and women around the country expressed the notion that if they solidified their relationship with a ceremony, their children, current or planned for, natural or adopted, would feel more like they were part of a traditional or "real" family. That ring on your finger or that blessing from a rabbi holds an incredible amount of sway when starting a family of your own. Guys have told us that, after a ceremony, their children felt more comfortable calling each partner "Dad." The same goes for women, who are much more likely to be in a situation where one partner already has kids from a previous marriage. Once a "marriage" is celebrated, the children feel much more comfortable calling their new mother "Mom." Having a wedding celebration will not solve all of your domestic issues—children will undoubtedly face those times in their lives when other kids ask why "Suzie has two moms"—but it's certainly a step in the right direction.

There's another reason, however, that we suspect more and more gay couples are deciding to wed. Traditionally, men and women are taught at a very young age that, someday, they'll meet the man or woman of their dreams, fall madly in love, get married, and have a family. This ideal isn't just a theory; it's expected. When parents and teachers and friends and relatives speak of this future, they speak of it in wondrous terms, the "rock" on which society rests and, most important, the single most critical criterion for becoming an adult.

So when these same children realize and accept that they are gay, many are torn not just by the immediate challenges—coming out, facing prejudice—but also by the other obstacles to fitting in that they will have to face. For many, this starts as early as high school, when other kids are dreaming about that first kiss, cheerleading and football practice, and the prom—all rites of passage in high school. True, many of you did participate in those activities, but most likely under the guise of a "normal" student. In other words, if you wanted to be a contributing member of society, you had to lie.

Marriage isn't all that different. While college tends to be a bit easier for gay men and women to cope with, not to mention a time to experiment—images of frat guys waking up with each other after beer blasts, and sorority sisters French-kissing as "practice" abound in coming-out stories—postgraduation life focuses more on the prospect of commitment. It's often the first time gays and lesbians have to come to terms with their sexuality on every level. Sadly, the desire to marry, to have children, and to be offered what has been, indeed, promised to them keeps many men and women in the closet for years. They often get married, have children, and keep their true sexuality hidden from their spouses, their families, and, to the extent that it's possible, themselves.

Gay weddings—and when they become legal, gay marriages—are the first step toward allowing homosexuals the opportunity to lead "traditional lives." One of the most ironic things about the gay-marriage controversy is that this so-called scandalous and radical movement is, for many gay couples, a desire to be anything but scandalous and radical. Furthermore, the most outspoken opponents of same-sex unions are the same people who generally label homosexuals "degenerates" or "perverts," and who never tire of stereotyping gay men and women as promiscuous beings whose only goal in life is to have as many sex partners as possible. Gay men and women who seek commitment ceremonies, whether through civil unions, domestic partnerships, or just a walk down the aisle, simply want what they are entitled to—a husband, a wife, a home, a family. And they're on their way.

Dreams Really Do Come True

And they lived happily ever after is one of those expressions we've all heard since childhood. It's associated with the princes and princesses in those wonderful fairy tales where, after a long series of trials and tribulations, the couple finally unite for all eternity, with a castle for a home and birds chirping around their heads.

While this certainly describes Gay Days at Disneyland, to a certain extent it probably describes the two of you. You've made the commitment to have a wedding, you want to spend the rest of your lives together, and you've been through your own trials and tribulations, fights and doubts, perhaps even a breakup or two.

However well intentioned those fairy-tale notions are, they've left out the

"One of the most ironic things about the gay-marriage controversy is that this so-called scandalous and radical movement is, for many gay couples, a desire to be anything but scandalous and radical."

details. In short, you have to have a plan. One of the things most couples, gay or straight, realize after deciding to wed is that they have no idea how to proceed. They're aware that they have to pick a date and location, and they know they have to figure out who's coming, and that guests will probably expect something to eat and drink. As the wedding planning begins, however, a million other questions start swirling around their heads. Should it be a big ceremony? When do we book a caterer? How do we go about writing the invitations?

Since you're a gay couple venturing into uncharted territory, it's likely that you've got even more questions, and fewer resources to turn to. Who leads during the first dance? Who makes the first toast? Do your lesbian attendants have to wear dresses, even if, for some of them, it will be the first time they've worn a gown since the high school prom (ironically, the same night they realized they were lesbians)?

Not to worry: What everyone has in common while planning a wedding is that, no matter what route they go, whether a traditional church wedding with two hundred guests or a backyard bash with only twenty close friends, is that they want to do it right. They want to make sure everyone has a good time, and that they understand the proper etiquette so that no one is offended. Most important, they want it to be a beautiful affair that everyone, not just the two of them, remembers for years to come.

All these issues will be addressed in the upcoming chapters. What's important to know now is that while planning might seem mind-blowing at first, you'll discover that if you stick to a schedule and devote a certain amount of time each day to your ceremony, you'll do just fine. And even though there seem to be ten million bridal magazines at your local bookstore, not to mention zillions of websites, it's really the meat and potatoes that you need to understand, and that is what this book is all about. Mainstream bridal books can be extremely helpful, and even gay people look at them for ideas. However, you should know that, while who leads the recessional at a Protestant ceremony as opposed to a Jewish affair might take up an entire chapter in a traditional wedding book, it's very unlikely the issue will be as imperative in a gay wedding. Also, many women who read bridal publications are doing so mainly to look at the ad pages for wedding-dress ideas, as opposed to the wedding tips inside.

You're also going to discover that, though planning a wedding is complicated and stressful, there's no reason it can't also be fun. Remember, this is the one time in your life that you get to be the star of your very own show. Bask in the attention. Part of the reason women dream about their weddings when they are still little girls is that they know that for a short period of time, everything is going to be about them. There's nothing wrong with that; this is your day and your celebration. As a gay man or woman, it's quite possible you never had this notion—gay weddings have only recently begun to step into the limelight. As much as this day is about solidifying your relationship to the world, there's also a tiny part of you that probably wants what the rest of society takes for granted; that clichéd but true notion that you are embarking on "the most special time of your life."

Try this experiment: Next time you're surrounded by a group of gay people—at your favorite bar, your weekly support group, any gym in Manhattan—open up this book so all can see you reading it. You'll be amazed at how many people come up to you to congratulate you, offer advice, share their own stories, and ask you the inevitable, "How are you going to wear your hair?" Male or female, you'll finally be treated like the queen you really are.

Two, Close for Comfort

A couple of things you need to do right away: Sit down with your partner and decide who's going to be in charge of what. In traditional wedding lore, the woman plans the wedding with lots of help from Mom, while the man says, "Just let me know what time I'm supposed to show up." The bride's family pays for the ceremony, while the groom's parents take care of the honeymoon and the rehearsal dinner. According to custom, the bride originally didn't even help plan the honeymoon. The man took care of all that.

Luckily, heterosexual unions are starting to break free from such rigid rules. Men are becoming more involved with wedding planning, both partners are planning the honeymoon, and couples often pay for the wedding themselves.

Ironically, this is one area where you actually have an advantage over heterosexual couples. You're not bound by any of these (frankly) silly and outdated conventions. While heterosexual society is slowly waking up to the idea that a wedding should be planned by the two people having it, homosexual society doesn't really have an option. True, some of you might ask Mom and Dad for financial help, but it's not expected of them to contribute. That, like every other stage of planning, is completely up to you.

Before you delve into this book, we strongly suggest that the two of you set a day aside to go over how you want to proceed. A few helpful hints:

- *Invest in wedding-planning software.* A variety of sites, including fivestar software.com, weddingsoft.com, frogwaresoftware.com, and smartwedding .com, offer software for between twenty-five and fifty dollars. These programs include options for budget organization, stationery design, checklists, guest-list management, and seating charts. Unfortunately, they do not currently make the software offered on these sites for Mac users, who'll need a Windows emulator to install the program.

  As an alternative, you can try the Mac-friendly essentialweddingplanner .com software, which includes a seating chart and vendor/guest management options for about twenty dollars. Both PC and Mac users who don't want to deal with software downloads can try the Web-based weddingtracker.com, which allows you to organize your invitations, RSVPs, and guest list online for about twenty dollars (for a year's subscription), or ezweddingplanner.com, a free Web-based wedding planner.

  If you don't already have a personal digital assistant (PDA), consider purchasing one to help you plan your big day. Your basic PDA usually includes an address book, date book, clock, to-do list, memo pad, notepad, calculator, and palm desktop software. More advanced multimedia features for PDAs include wireless telephone, voice recorder, digital camera, MP3, and Internet capabilities. Prices range from around a hundred dollars to as much as nine hundred, depending on the features the model offers. Check out shop.bizrate.com for a comprehensive comparison of available PDAs.

Not a computer geek? Invest in a simple notebook, or head to your local bookstore's bridal section and purchase a planner specifically designed for keeping track of your wedding needs. Some of you might prefer writing notes on the back of matchbook covers. We've also tried to make things easier for you by putting in checklists throughout the book. Like everything else, the golden rule is to use whatever's easiest for you.

- *Set a schedule every day for both of you to get together and go over planning.* For instance, if one of you is a morning person and the other a night owl, don't fool yourselves and think some sort of wedding magic will change all of that. Plan to talk daily—for instance, each night right after dinner. The important thing is to make sure it's a time that both of you agree on and that both of you can make each day. And if this means you'll have to spend less time at the gym each night, or skip your daily History Channel fix, get over it. Your body will understand, and history repeats itself.

- *Accept the fact that you're going to argue.* Ryan O'Neal and Ali MacGraw in *Love Story* were wrong when they said that "Love means never having to say you're sorry." In fact, love means apologizing a lot! Stress causes people to fight, and the sooner you accept this, the sooner you'll learn how to resolve these conflicts. And the sooner you make up, the sooner you get to have make-up sex.

- *Delegate tasks.* Decide which one of you is suited for which jobs. Whoever has the best head for business should take care of financial transactions, including haggling with wedding vendors. Similarly, the better diplomat should be the one to deal with friends and relatives and any issues that may arise in that arena. If you're both floral freaks, now's the time to confront this and learn the art of compromise (if one of you loves roses, the other tulips, go with orchids, the second choice for both of you—like married life, it's all about the compromise). Do agree that no decisions will be made without the other's consent. You don't want to start your new gay life by keeping secrets; that way of thinking ended when you let go of the Fire Island or Provincetown share.

None of you reading this book needs a lesson on bravery, but you will have to deal with the unknown. Emily Post doesn't give tips on gay receiving-line etiquette, and there are a lot of factors in your wedding that you can't simply ask your parents about. In the following chapters, we'll address many of those concerns. We'll inform you of traditional wedding customs and suggest alternative ideas that may be more suitable for a same-sex wedding. There are also examples of real gay weddings, to give you an idea of what other couples have gone through, what choices they made, and special ways they made their own celebrations sparkle.

The one thing you can never forget is that no matter what you read and what advice people give you, this is your wedding, your money, and your dream. Do whatever you want. One of my beefs with wedding "experts" is when they tell you point-blank what you can and cannot do at your celebration. To give tips is one thing; to tell you no is quite another. Traditional bridal publications love to point out that Jennifer Aniston and Brad Pitt made a major faux pas by incorporating corny vows into their ceremony. Personally, we think that if Jen felt that making Brad his favorite banana milk shakes was important enough for her to include in her vows, more power to her. Similarly, Barbra Streisand's floor-length veil and—gasp!—white dress at her second wedding, to James Brolin, brought cries of "Yentl's Gone Mental" by the wedding press. Wear white, off-white, or nothing *but* a veil if that's your true wedding wish. We can give you advice, but only you can decide what to do with it. When in doubt, always go with your instincts.

Remember, you're not alone: Thousands of man–man and woman–woman weddings take place each year, and you're all in this together. The fun part is that, by deciding on having a gay wedding, you're at the forefront of a whole new world. Gay weddings are in the Genesis stage, and you're right there along Adam and Steve and Vanessa and Eve. Together, what we don't know, we'll figure out. What we've been denied in the past, we'll demand for our future. We can't turn back the clock; gay weddings are here to stay. Like others before you, you, too, have a dream—one that will never die. When you put down this book and say "I do," that dream will forever be reality.

And you thought coming out the first time was difficult. Now that you're engaged, you've got to tell Mom and Dad, sisters and brothers, and all your close friends and relatives. Don't put this off. Once your friends see that twinkle in your eye and realize it's not from laser eye surgery, they're going to get suspicious. For some of you, telling parents may not pose a problem. If you've been with your partner for a long period of time, and your parents accept the relationship, they'll most likely be delighted by the news. As with any traditional couple, it's nice if you tell them over dinner or brunch, in a comfortable setting, perhaps a favorite restaurant or at home; whether you think it's appropriate to tell them alone or together is entirely up to you.

If your parents have never met your partner, or they don't approve of your relationship, this is going to be a trickier situation. Hence, it's best to get it over with as soon as possible. (However, if you anticipate problems, do not tell them immediately. You want to bask in your engagement as long as possible before the unpleasant realities set in. Wait a week or so and, in the meantime, lavish yourself and your partner.)

If it's simply a matter of them not knowing your partner (say, if he or she lives in another part of the country), perhaps you could arrange a time for everyone to meet before the wedding. If that's physically impossible—your parents are ailing and can't travel, for example—arrange a conference call. Even if they don't approve of your ceremony, your parents will be much more comfortable about your wedding once they've "met" your partner. Think of your situation in terms of politics: When two countries don't get along, the best approach is to start talking. It's when communication ends that all hell breaks loose.

However you choose to approach the situation, make sure your parents know before the rest of the world does. If your relationship is already strained as a result of your sexuality, it's only going to get worse if your parents find out you're hitched through the gossipy next-door neighbor. Remember that infamous scene in *Ordinary People* when Mary Tyler Moore's character finds out from a friend that her son has quit the swim team? Tell Mom first and you'll both make it after all.

Finally, if your parents don't know that you're gay, let alone about to commit to someone of the same sex, you've now got a great reason to come out of the closet. They're going to find out soon enough (and guess what?—on some level, they probably already know). The only way to look at a situation like this is to compare it to doing a chore you despise, like filing your taxes or having a root canal: You dread the process, but you're going to feel much better about yourself when the job's done. If that sounds like a simplification, it is. However, a tough problem like this requires tough love: You can't live a happy, fulfilled life, let alone one with a partner, without being honest about your sexuality. It isn't fair to your parents, it's certainly not fair to your partner, and, most important, it's not fair to yourself.

If you're not ready to come out, take the time to evaluate if you're prepared for the realities having a wedding will bring. You might find that you need to be more comfortable with your sexuality before you're ready to make a commitment in front of the world.

Children Will Listen . . . as Will Friends, as Will Co-Workers

Follow pretty much the same rule with close friends and relatives as you do with your parents. Granted, your younger brother Joey might not need a conference call with his new brother-in-love, but he, too, should hear the news from you as soon as possible. Depending on how young your sibling is, there could be the added stress of being teased at school or other social activities about the lesbian sister and her lover. Make sure your sib knows that you've met the person you intend to spend the rest of your life with, and that this is in every sense of the word a real marriage. Put this off, or avoid the subject altogether, and the union might not be taken seriously. This would also be a great time to ask your baby sister Linda to play a major role in the wedding.

If either one of you has children, and assuming you have at least partial custody, immediately plan a time to sit down with them, alone, to give them the news. Your children are the last people in your life who should hear about your wedding from someone else. Depending on your situation and your children's ages, they might have a lot of concerns about the nuptials. Go over any fears they have about adjusting to a new life with gay parents, and let them know that both of you will be there for them during this time. Just like any other kids adjusting to remarriage, they might not immediately like their new mom or new dad. Give it time.

Whether or not you tell office mates or your boss is, of course, up to you, and will most likely depend on how out you are at work. If you do plan on telling them, you need to understand that they'll be wondering if they're invited—and don't be surprised if some assume they are. So before you send that mass office e-mail around, make this decision with your partner.

The standard etiquette for co-workers is that you either invite them all or just your immediate supervisor. No matter how close you are to individual office mates, you're going to hurt a lot of feelings if you single out just one or two of them. Similarly, do you really want to invite that guy in sales whom you've never actually been introduced to and who never washes after flushing? Remember, he'll be touching the food! Whichever route you choose, it's always good to have a response ready if someone who's not invited asks. "We'd love to invite everyone, but it's going to be a simple ceremony with close friends and family" is the diplomatic course. "You're a lush with a bad wig" is best saved for holiday gatherings.

To clear things up, you should also immediately tell your boss that all wedding preparations will take place either during lunch hours or before or after work. (In other words, lie.)

Length of Engagement

This is the time to decide how long you need and/or want to plan the wedding. It's important to figure this out now, because so many of the next steps you take will be affected by the length of your engagement. Traditionally, couples are engaged for approximately a year, which gives you plenty of time to make all the necessary preparations. (As you will see in the Wedding Countdown Calendar on pages 217–220, this book is tailored for a twelve-month planning process. Add or subtract tasks according to your own routine.)

Some factors to keep in mind when scheduling your wedding:

- *Indoor/outdoor ceremony.* If you envision a garden party or beach affair, and you get engaged in February, you'll probably want to put off your wedding for more than a year, so that you don't end up reading your vows under rain or snow or sleet or hail. Don't try to be Superman and put the affair together in two months.
- *Availability of sites.* It's a fact of life: The hot spots book up quickly, whether they be restaurants, banquet halls, hotels, or nude beaches. Those nice folks at Tavern on the Green aren't going to automatically book you for the date and time you choose just because you're having a wedding. The longer your engagement, the better your chances of booking your dream site on the date of your choice.
- *Married-life adjustments.* If you don't live together, figure out how much time it will take to find a new place, or for one of you to move out of your old home. If this involves a job transfer, you might want to extend your engagement a few months. If you have children, and they are going to be uprooted, plan your wedding so as to not interrupt their schooling.

The Next Best Thing

Finally, there's one last thing you need to know before you start wedding planning. Next to your lover, the most important thing to bring to your ceremony is the understanding that something will go wrong. Even if the two of you are the savviest planners on the planet, and you've devoted seven days a week for the past two years to preparing a wedding that goes off without a hitch, it'll never happen. Like death and taxes, wedding snafus are part of life.

Once you accept this fact, it enables you to enjoy the day to its fullest. For no matter what occurs—the flowers are wilted, the officiant's late, your mother gets lost on the way—all that's really important is that the two of you are together, in love, and standing in front of the world to celebrate your union. The rest is just the icing on the wedding cake.

Have a gay old time.

We the People of the [...]

a more perfect [...]

for the common defense [...]

to ourselves and [...] of America

Two

LOVE
AND
"MARRIAGE"

John & Michael

WHO: John Senago, forty-three, and Michael Arden, forty-five.

WHEN: Sunday, April 28, 2002.

WHERE: The Union Station, downtown Los Angeles. An outdoor, courtyard affair in an art deco building for two hundred guests.

GAY/Q: The couple wore "off-the-expensive-rack" designer Mexican wedding shirts, slacks, and sandals.

THANK GOODNESS A HOUSE DIDN'T DROP ON HER: The officiant was a witch. "She's a good witch," says Michael. "She predicted I would meet John."

CRISSCROSS: John's Catholic, Michael's Jewish, so they read scripture and incorporated the breaking of the glass.

KODAK MOMENT: A guest screamed out, "I finally get to see a gay wedding before I die!"

RHODA MOMENT: They rode to and from the ceremony on the Los Angeles Metro.

SO LA: Three different caterers, five hundred tamales, five cakes, and six salads.

SO DOWN SOUTH: Margaritas and a mariachi band started the festivities.

A RING TO REMEMBER: Michael proposed to John at the top of the Empire State Building. "It was two weeks after 9/11, and it was really hard to get the ring past security without John knowing it."

EASTERN STANDARD: A dinner the night before for forty close friends and family at Yamashiro, a Japanese restaurant in the Hollywood Hills.

WHAT THEY OVERCAME: The ceremony was held on the same day as Fiesta LA, a huge Latino festival right next to their ceremony site. Thousands of onlookers watched in wonder. Says Michael, "We didn't know what to expect, but the crowds were great. Who can deny love when they see it?"

STRAIGHT FROM THE HEART: They couldn't resist the traditional custom of feeding each other cake.

MAKEOVER TIPS: "A limo would have been nice," says Michael.

HONEYMOON G-SPOT: A few days in Mykonos, then off to Venice, birthplace of John's relatives.

PARTING WORDS: "If I couldn't commit to a partner in front of people," Michael says, "it would have been easy to bail at some point. I think about that on days that are not as great as others. That's part of the reason marriages last."

The term *marriage,* according to the Defense of Marriage Act (DOMA) signed by President Clinton in 1996, means "a legal union between one man and one woman as husband and wife." President George W. Bush shortened that terminology further, stating that "marriage is between a man and woman." And the Vatican, in an effort to clear up any confusion over the genders in question, wrote in 2003 that "marriage exists solely between a man and woman."

Reading all this, the debate over same-sex marriage seems, at first, moot. After all, with such a clear-cut male–female definition, what's the point in even pretending that marriage is something that should extend to gay and lesbian couples? Perhaps it's time for all the protesters to pack up, let the folks in Washington and Rome tend to more important matters, and return home to their significant other, partner, lover, boyfriend, girlfriend, or better half. "Marriage" is for straight people. Simply put, you can't have your cake and call it legal, too.

But there's another definition that's conspicuously absent in these succinct, if not exactly profound, interpretations of marriage. Ironically, it's the definition that, as children, we are taught is more important than any other. Marriage, we've been brought up to believe, is a "commitment of love."

If this is true, and "happily ever after" is something that as adults we both expect and deserve, then the same-sex-marriage opponents are going about it all wrong. They should spend less time threatening legal action and constitutional amendments, and more time trying to prove that Chuck and Tyrone or Sally and Jane are not truly in love.

Furthermore, while people who are morally threatened by gay marriage scramble to find legal challenges to keep their institution technically heterosexual, those planning gay weddings are doing so on the emotional impulse that marriage is all about the love they share, and making that love visible in the eyes of family, friends, even church. The very fact that gay couples still want to have weddings even though marriage is illegal demonstrates very strongly that gay weddings are a product of love. If anyone can find a better reason than that to have a ceremony, we urge them to speak their piece.

This is not to suggest that gay-marriage proponents don't care about the legal ramifications of wedded bliss. On the contrary, one of the main arguments in support of extending marriage rights to gays and lesbians is that they'll be afforded the same benefits and freedoms that lawfully married couples receive. This, as everybody interviewed for this book will attest, is a natural progression of civil rights—the right to equality. (A right, it should be noted, that extends to *not* getting married as well. There are many gay men and women who have no interest in wedlock, because they see it as either an outdated, failed institution or society's biggest and oldest discriminatory club. Once again, this is merely equal rights at play—just ask those straight couples who've been together for years and would sooner have a lobotomy than a marriage.)

As the struggle to make gay marriage legal continues, however, gay *weddings* are already here. Wherever you stand on the political side of this issue, you should have a basic understanding of the current same-sex-union laws in this country and the rest of the world. You might discover that filing for domestic partnership can indeed help you in sickness and in health, or that the cost of a plane ticket to get married in Canada isn't worth the objections you'll receive in your hometown.

For better or worse, then, a basic rundown:

First off, just to remind you of what Bill, George, and Rome left out, when two straight people get married they are automatically qualified for various federal and state rights, including, among other things, health insurance, adoption, pensions, taxes, Social Security, inheritance, and hospital/health-care decision making.

As of this printing, marriage between a same-sex couple is illegal in all fifty states, thirty-six of which have passed the Defense of Marriage Act, which protects states from having to honor out-of-state same-sex marriages or civil unions. What this means is that, although Linda and Janette may have been together for twenty years, if one of them dies, the survivor does not receive Social Security benefits. On the other hand, their just-married next-door neighbors, Joe and Nancy, would benefit in similar circumstances.

All queer and straight eyes are on Massachusetts, after the state supreme court ruled in November 2003 that banning same-sex marriage is unconstitutional. This decision could, in effect, make the state the first to legalize same-sex marriage. The struggle looks to be a long one, however, with both the Bush administration and conservative groups vowing to block passage by any means necessary, for instance, with the Bush-supported constitutional amendment banning gay marriage. At the time of this printing, all we can say is, stay tuned.

In 2000 Vermont passed laws creating what's called a *civil union,* which gives gay and lesbian partners the same state benefits afforded to married couples. Under this law, Lionel and Kevin have access to the same health-insurance benefits as their married Vermont neighbors Amy and John. Because property rights fall under federal jurisdiction, however, should Lionel or Kevin die, the surviving partner would have no property rights, while Amy or John would still have a home. As of this printing, civil unions are not recognized out of state. Many gay couples have civil unions in Vermont purely as a symbolic gesture.

In California, if a gay couple files for *domestic partnership* with the secretary of state's office, they have access to improved disability coverage and sick leave, inheritance rights, employer-sponsored health-care coverage, and medical decision-making authority. In January 2004, New Jersey enacted a domestic partnership bill that gives same-sex couples health insurance benefits, property rights, and other survivor's benefits. In addition, New Jersey will recognize domestic partnerships in other states. Outside California about fifty cities and counties offer domestic-partnership registries (go to the Human Rights Campaign's website at hrc.org/familynet for a list). Though loosely defined as "spousal benefits," the actual implications of domestic partnerships vary: Connecticut law requires that domestic partners draw notarized and witnessed statements or a power of attorney in order to be eligible for rights in medical emergencies, old age, and death, as well as rights for crime victims. Hawaii offers limited state rights for any two individuals—blood relatives, friends, and same-sex couples. Rights such as inheritance without a will, wrongful death, hospital-visitation and health-care decisions, property rights, and protection under domestic violence laws are included. However, the laws' provisions for health care, life insurance, and retirement all expired in 1999 and have not been renewed. The District of Columbia gives domestic partners the same rights as legal family members: Hospital-visitation benefits, decision-making ability regarding remains, including partners on health-care plans, and annual leave for birth or adoption are all offered to same-sex couples.

Same-sex marriage was legalized in Holland in April 2001, and the country has eliminated all references to gender in marriage and adoption laws. Following that ruling, Belgium approved a bill in 2002 that recognizes same-sex marriage. Unlike Holland's bill, Belgium's is open to people of any nationality. The Belgian bill, however, does not allow gay couples to adopt. The third country to recognize same-sex marriage is our neighbor to the north. In June 2003 Prime Minister Jean Chrétien of Canada enacted a national policy that extends marriage to gay couples. There are no residence requirements; should you file for divorce, however, you need to be a yearlong resident.

Additional countries that offer same-sex couples benefits through registered partnerships or similar laws include Denmark, Finland, France, Germany, Greenland, Iceland, Norway, and Sweden. Parts of Africa and Latin America, as well as Israel, are debating the issue of same-sex unions. Log on to http://www.glad.org/Publications/CivilRightProject/OP5-aroundtheworld.shtml for a breakdown of the benefits these and other countries provide.

CANADIAN MARRIAGE

If you're not a Canadian resident, the most complicated aspect of getting married in Canada is that it has to take place in the province of British Columbia or Ontario. Other than that, it's as easy as a honeymoon in Vegas. You must be at least nineteen years of age (anyone younger needs the consent of both parents), and there are no residency requirements. The license is valid for three months. You can choose either a civil or a religious ceremony. (For a step-by-step guide, go to the British Columbia Vital Statistics Agency at www.vs.gov.bc.ca/marriage/howto.html.) A same-sex Canadian marriage is not recognized in the United States.

CIVIL UNIONS

It's almost as easy for Jerry and Ben to have a civil union in Vermont as it is to visit Ben & Jerry's ice cream factory. As in Canada, you only need to be nineteen years of age. Once you've received your license, it's applicable for sixty days. Look up city or town clerks in Vermont's white pages, or go to gay-civil-unions.com for guidelines, as well as suggestions on places to wed and ceremony options. There are no residency requirements for a civil union in Vermont.

DOMESTIC PARTNERSHIP

To file for domestic partnership, call your county clerk's office about forms and procedures. As noted above, domestic partnership can vary a great deal depending on where you live, so be sure to check out all the advantages (and disadvantages) filing will give you. Remember, although Canadian marriages and Vermont civil unions are not recognized outside those areas, some states, cities, or companies might honor your new status. Make sure to read up on the latest developments; visit hrc.org for more information.

Divorce and Dissolution

Just because an affair is gay doesn't mean it's going to have a happy ending. Should you go to Canada or Vermont to make it legal, you'll have to return to either spot if you want to terminate your union. To obtain a Canadian divorce or a Vermont dissolution, one of you has to live there for a year. So while that Vermont civil union might be symbolic for nonresidents, the dissolution is not. This is one more example of the differences between civil unions and straight marriage. Heterosexuals can marry in one state and get divorced in another; gay couples can't. The negative ramifications are obvious. On the upside, it's one more reason to truly focus on how important making your union legal is for the two of you.

Terminating a domestic partnership is much easier. One partner has to file a notice of termination with the city clerk. Any third party affected, such as a benefits program, must receive a copy of the termination within sixty days of the dissolution.

The Adoption Option

For those of you hoping to have children after you wed, here are a few facts about adoption procedures.

While many states allow gay couples to adopt, New Jersey was the first to enact a law allowing same-sex couples to do so jointly. That bill, which passed in 1997, prohibits couples seeking to be adoptive parents from being discriminated against due to sexual orientation. In California, under domestic-partnership laws, same-sex couples can apply for adoption according to the same procedures as stepparents.

On the flip side, Florida bans gay individuals and couples from adopting altogether, while Utah and Mississippi ban same-sex couples from adopting. In these two states, should you choose to have children, one of you will need to adopt as an individual. However, it's highly unlikely that a judge in these states will grant adoption to a homosexual.

Most other states allow same-sex couples to adopt, though it is not statewide policy and, ultimately, depends on individual judges. For specific adoption laws in your state, go to hrc.org/familynet. According to a report issued by the Evan B. Donaldson Adoption Institute, as of 2003, 60 percent of adoption agencies accept applications from gays and lesbians, and 40 percent have placed children with homosexuals.

If you're turned down for adoption as a couple, you should consider individual adoption or second-parent adoption. Under second-parent adoption, only one partner petitions to adopt. After that adoption is processed, the second partner adopts the child as well. Second-parent adoption is also commonly used for gay couples when one partner already has a child. With second-parent adoption, the two partners have equal legal standing as parents and share the same rights that biological parents have over children.

If one of you already has a child and second-parent adoption is unavailable, you can prepare either a custody agreement or co-parenting agreement, which states how the child's welfare will be taken care of, what conduct and behavior is acceptable and unacceptable in the relationship, and what actions will take place in the event of a breakup. Any couple can make this agreement legal provided they have two witnesses; though it's not required, you should also have the document notarized.

Words to Live By . . .

Remember when you first brought home a lover to your parents and he or she was introduced to everyone as your "friend"? No matter how many times the word was used, it always seemed to have quotation marks around it. You'd be celebrating some holiday or another, and when June and Rick from next door popped in, Mom would turn to them and say, "I'd like you to meet Cecilia's 'friend' Susan."

Inevitably, Susan would look even more uncomfortable than you, Dad would change the subject to something less awkward, like the Middle East conflict, and June and Rick would try to grasp the reason behind the strange intonation of "friend," which sounded oddly like Susan might be a CIA agent or a serial killer holding the family hostage.

Hopefully, you and your family have progressed on the "What do I call him/her?" question. Still, as you approach your wedding day, don't be surprised if the issue resurfaces. Friends and relatives will want to make sure they address your partner correctly, and it's up to you to let them know what you prefer. Insisting that loved ones decide for themselves is not only placing an unnecessary onus on them, but might also result in you and your soul mate being "friends" for life.

Here, some optimal ways to communicate your new monikers:

- *Let your families do the talking.* If loved ones are involved in wedding planning, give them the thumbs-up to tell guests what you'd like to be called. For instance, if Sis decides to throw you an engagement party, have her remind people that after the wedding you've decided to use the term *partners*. This way, when your best college buddy walks through the door, she can immediately say, "I'm just dying to meet your partner." Some guests might feel awkward asking you the question directly.

- *Speak for yourself.* Start using your monikers immediately. At parties, dinners, anywhere you're around people you'll be in contact with after the wedding, make a point of introducing him or her appropriately. "Hey, Kyle, have you met my soon-to-be-spouse, Lance?" works as an opener. You can also apply this technique solo: "I really wanted my spouse, Renée, to be here tonight, but she's busy with ceramics class."

- *In the cards.* Use any correspondence that coincides with your engagement period as a chance to show off your new nouns. "Dear Judith, My partner, Nicolle, and I want to thank you for that wonderful 'Meet the Exes' dinner party last week" certainly lets everyone know you've moved beyond the "friends" stage. E-mail is another great place to get the names across: "Dear BeerBear, My fiancé, Geoff, and I are sorry to say we can't make your annual Russian River preparty keg blast, as we'll be attending the annual Protein-Plus Expo that weekend. Love, SmoothNRipped."

TERMS OF ENDEARMENT

Need help deciding what to call each other after the wedding? Here's what other couples have decided.

Interestingly, most people interviewed said they use *partner* around friends and co-workers, and *husband* or *wife* at home. Since gay marriage is not legally recognized, perhaps the latter terms seem inappropriate in formal circles. Regardless, if it's comfortable for you, by all means praise your new husband or wife in front of everyone within earshot. Gay matrimony may be illegal, but traditional marriage phrases are not.

On an added note, nary a couple said they call each other *partner* when they're relaxing at home. Then again, "My partner will get on the phone just as soon as he makes the martinis" does sound more like a merger than a marriage.

The next most popular term is *spouse*. Couples like this term because it leaves no doubt that a union has been formed, but steers away from the traditional ramifications of *husband* and *wife*. Given the fact that both men and women can use this term, it gains added points for being inclusive.

Still, there are couples who, after being wed, go with nicknames like *significant other, better half,* or *lover,* usually terms that were long established before the wedding. On the flip side, everyone we spoke with who used to address each other as *boyfriend* or *girlfriend* has since disposed of those "not-serious-enough" names. Chances are, if you've had a wedding, you're no longer just "going steady."

Finally, we're happy to report that not a single wedded couple referred to their lifelong partner as *friend* after the wedding day. Now go tell Mom and Dad.

THE NAME CHANGE

It's not just for heterosexuals anymore: Gay couples are changing their names, too. And just like your straight married friends, the options are numerous. In heterosexual matrimony, it's most common for women to change their surnames to their husbands'. (Guys, pay attention; you'll need to figure out who's who.) Recently, there's been a trend for married couples to form a hyphenated last name of both surnames; also popular is forming a hybrid name. In gay translation, this means that Julie Smith and Selena Rogers might change their names to Julie and Selena Smith-Rogers or Selena and Julie Rogers-Smith. A hybrid would read something like Julie and Selena Smithro.

Unlike straight couples, who simply sign their new names on the marriage license, you'll have to contact a lawyer or the county court to find out the correct procedure—it varies from state to state (go to soyouwanna.com for a complete list of rules and regulations). And just so you know, those pet porn nicknames you've given each other won't work in the real world. It's against the law to use foul language when legally changing your name.

Once you've taken care of the legal issue, make sure your new name gets out to the right places—start by contacting the Department of Motor Vehicles and the Social Security Administration; official documents with your new name will make it much easier to change it elsewhere. Necessary changes include your passport, the IRS, and medical records. It's up to you to decide if the people at *Us Weekly* should have a record of your new moniker.

Finally, before you apply for new joint credit cards, remember that bad credit on either side reflects on both of you. So if one of you has always paid your balance in full and the other thinks a call from the bank signals that it's time to pay your bill, you might want to rethink your card coupling—either that or let the more organized of the two of you handle all bills.

HOLIDAY . . . CELEBRATION?

Think deciding what to call your union won't be complicated? When the *New York Times* began announcing same-sex ceremonies in 2002, it actually changed the name of the Sunday "Weddings" section to "Weddings/Celebrations," thus alleviating the problem of making a distinction. You, too, might find choosing a name for your union complicated. Some couples think *commitment ceremony* sounds demeaning—less than a marriage in the eyes of the public. The polar opposite response is from people who shudder at the thought of calling their union *wedding,* a ritual they view exclusively for straight people.

Don't stress: The good news is that you can call it whatever you want:

wedding, commitment, union, partnership, exchange of vows, fag-fest, or lesbian love-in. There are no rules. The bad news? Should you choose to go with *marriage,* don't expect your local paper to honor that title in its announcement unless you've run off to Canada to tie the knot.

Keeping the Faith

If you ever wonder why same-sex ceremonies cause such a commotion, keep in mind the old adage that religion and politics are two of the most dangerous topics to bring up in mixed company. The very nature of the term *gay wedding* brings both subjects to the forefront. That's why, now that we've covered, be it ever so briefly, the legal climate of same-sex unions, we thought we'd plunge straight into the religious aspects.

Luckily, you're among friends.

Of the world's five major religions—Christianity, Judaism, Islam, Hinduism, and Buddhism—only the latter two don't condemn homosexuality. Islam takes the worst stance, labeling homosexuality a perversion, but conservative interpreters of the Bible don't have either the will or the grace to accept gays or lesbians, either. Further, none of these religions supports same-sex unions. Those who argue otherwise are probably counting denominations within religious bodies, not the official statements from these faiths, that is, same-sex marriages that are performed by many Reform Jewish rabbis, but not by Orthodox Jewish rabbis. According to a study by the Catholic University of America Marriage Law Project (marriagelaw.cua.edu/religion.htm), fewer than 2 percent of religious bodies in the United States support same-sex marriage.

Here's a basic rundown of the major religions' positions on homosexuality and same-sex marriage.

CHRISTIANITY

POSITION OF THE CATHOLIC CHURCH: Marriage is between a man and a woman. Homosexuality is a disorder and should not be acted upon. Those afflicted should be loved and accepted but expected to remain celibate.

POSITION OF THE ORTHODOX CHURCH: Opposed to same-sex marriage.

POSITION OF THE PROTESTANT CHURCH: Opposed to same-sex marriage. This includes Anabaptists, Baptists, Episcopalians/Anglicans, Evangelical Quakers, Independent Evangelicals, Lutherans, Pentecostals, Reformed and Presbyterian, Seventh-day Adventists, and Wesleyans/Methodists. (Exceptions within the Protestant Church that support same-sex marriage include the Unitarian Universalist Association and the Universal Fellowship of Metropolitan Community Churches.)

POSITION OF THE CHURCH OF JESUS CHRIST OF LATTER-DAY SAINTS (MORMONS): Opposed to same-sex marriage and condemns homosexuality in church doctrine.

JUDAISM

POSITION OF ORTHODOX JUDAISM: Opposed to same-sex marriage. Jewish law forbids homosexual relations. You are accepted and loved as a homosexual, but must remain celibate.

POSITION OF CONSERVATIVE JUDAISM: Opposed to same-sex marriage but claims to be against homosexual discrimination and in favor of equal rights for gays and lesbians.

POSITION OF RECONSTRUCTIONIST JUDAISM: Supportive of same-sex marriage. Supports rabbis who choose to perform same-sex ceremonies.

POSITION OF REFORM JUDAISM: Supportive of same-sex civil marriages but divided on whether to preside over commitment ceremonies.

ISLAM

Against same-sex marriage. Homosexuality is a sin. It is a sick and unlawful deviation/perversion. Any homosexual can become a heterosexual.

BUDDHISM

There are no specific laws or rulings against homosexuality, and the Dalai Lama has neither condemned nor supported it.

HINDUISM

Marriage is viewed as an important social and religious duty between a man and a woman. Modern Hinduism generally views a homosexual orientation as a poor choice, as opposed to a genetic predisposition. Neo-Hindus take a stronger stance against the orientation. However, homosexuality is not specifically condemned in scripture.

From a philosophical point of view, if you want to find point-blank proof in the Bible that homosexuality is not a sin, go to the task with my blessing—and a lot of aspirin. Since there are as many interpretations of Bible passages, in as many different Bibles, as there are religions around the world, it's an argument you could spend eternity debating.

What is generally agreed upon, however, is that religion has, for the most part, been especially alienating for homosexuals. No one's going to blame you, then, if you never enter a house of worship, decide to sue your Sunday-school teacher for emotional duress, or only mention the Lord's name *in* vain.

Luckily, there are religious alternatives for gay people interested in keeping their religion. The inner peace and strength that faith can provide should never be denied, especially at such an important event as a wedding. Thank, well, whoever you like that within most religious denominations there are groups that are specifically for or accepting of homosexuals and gay marriage. Christianlesbians.com is an excellent site that offers a list of churches and congregations that are gay-friendly. It directs you state by state to the appropriate contact. Within all these denominations, you can be married by a church official. Once you've made the right contact, simply explain that you'd like to arrange a same-sex ceremony. (Before you venture away from your own church, however, talk to an official there. More and more religious leaders are becoming tolerant of same-sex unions, and will often agree to perform ceremonies.)

Most likely, you'll be required to meet with whoever's marrying you for counseling and ceremony planning. Your wedding will probably be structured around basic heterosexual procedures, though you can personalize and change elements to reflect your backgrounds and history by writing your own vows, choosing readings, including ethnic elements, and the like. Witnesses are usually required. Interfaith wedding issues often come into play as well. If that's the case for the two of you, state the situation ("I'm Muslim, he's a Jew") and ask how, besides getting wedding tips from watching *Funny Girl,* you can incorporate both your religions into the ceremony. You can also request a church official to bless your union even if you don't plan on having your ceremony in a house of worship. Chances are, however, you'll still have to meet for premarital counseling sessions.

INTERFAITH OPTIONS

There are two other popular routes to go with if you're having an interfaith ceremony. First, you can opt for co-officiants to bless your union. If a license is involved, such as with a civil union, only one of the officiants can sign it, so decide ahead of time which faith gets first billing. (A word of caution: Any officiant who tells you he or she is doubly ordained is lying. Steer clear of those who can't decide which side they preach for.) If you have children, or are planning to, this is a good time to discuss what religion, if any, you will raise them with. Years from now, you don't want them to be confused as they look back at the wedding video and see men in yarmulkes reciting Protestant vows. Also, take note ahead of time that if your officiant is unwilling to combine faiths, one of you might be required to convert.

Another option (and one that is especially appealing if you have trouble finding an officiant willing to combine faiths) is to have two ceremonies: either two religious weddings for two different faiths, or a secular ceremony followed by a religious one at a later date. It's an art of compromise commonly practiced in heterosexual weddings, and it has the added benefit of satisfying both sets of parents, should they be involved with planning and adamant about religious touches.

Set on having your wedding at your childhood house of worship? Don't automatically count on it. Since it's customary for the in-house holy person to officiate, he or she will have to be comfortable with your same-sex ceremony. Should that person not feel comfortable officiating, but have no personal issues with homosexual weddings, etiquette dictates that it's up to him or her to ask someone else to perform the duties.

NONDENOMINATIONAL WEDDINGS

Want your spiritual surroundings to be a day at the beach? Consider a nondenominational service. Strictly speaking, a nondenominational minister is someone who is familiar with all major religions and can incorporate any of them into your service without the constraints of having to hold your affair at a house of worship. You don't have to belong to any faith in order to go this route. Couples often choose nondenominational ceremonies because of past associations with religion they'd like to rekindle on this day, or to simply add an element of tradition into the service. A good place to start is the Unitarian Universalist Association, which welcomes people of all faiths and is a firm supporter of same-sex unions (www.uua.org or check your local yellow pages).

CIVIL SERVICES

If you're not religious, or you'd rather bypass such traditions as premarital counseling (those of you who've been together for ten years might find yourself saying, "Hey, if we've made it this far . . ."), or even if you'd simply like more freedom in how your ceremony is put together, consider a wedding presided over by a judge, a justice of the peace, or a county or court clerk. These ceremonies are usually performed at city hall, though you can ask for them to take place at another location, like your reception site. The good news is that, should you choose a court wedding, there are no rules. You can recite the lyrics from "I Touch Myself" for your vows if you'd like, and wear high-tops and tanks as wedding attire. On the downside, the space you recite your "I dos" in probably won't match Westminster Abbey. Remember, however, that even if your wedding takes place at city hall, you can still throw a reception for three hundred at the classiest restaurant in town. Call your county clerk's office for more information.

GETTING TO KNOW YOUR OFFICIANT

Just like finding a good therapist, the most important thing to remember when choosing your officiant is that you have to like him or her. After all, this is the person who will be solidifying your lifelong commitment, who might indeed be giving you premarital counseling, and who, if nothing else, will be a featured guest on your big day. Don't just settle on the first person who answers the phone. If, after you meet, you're uncomfortable with someone's personality, views on your relationship, heck, even taste in music, move on. You're putting your life in your officiant's hands, so to speak, and you want to trust him or her implicitly. Also, be sure to invite your officiant, along with his or her spouse or partner, to the rehearsal dinner if you are having one, as well as to the ceremony. If they are traveling to be at your wedding, it's customary to pay for transportation and lodgings.

NET-ESCAPE

If Joey Tribbiani could get ordained over the Internet to marry Monica and Chandler, believe me, so can you. For no charge (or five bucks if you send your information via snail mail), the Universal Life Church will ordain you within a few weeks (universalministries.com). Whether you worship Jesus, Allah, or Diana Ross (pre- or post-Supremes breakup), the church will give you its blessing, provided you give it the correct information. The most complicated question you'll probably encounter is gender—you can choose only one. It's a great way to reduce that religion stress *and* include a loved one in your ceremony. And that's what friends are for.

Three

BALANCING
THE
BUDGET

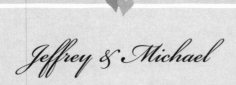

Jeffrey & Michael

WHO: Jeffrey Smythe, thirty, and Michael Collins-Smythe, thirty.

WHEN: Saturday, May 13, 2000.

WHERE: Ceremony at Christ Covenant Church in Atlanta, Georgia, reception for 150 people at an antebellum home nearby.

STYLE COUNCIL: Formal six o'clock wedding, followed by a reception an hour later. The grooms both wore black tie.

MEMBERS OF THE WEDDING: Sisters of each groom participated, along with six groomsmen and two best men, all in formalwear.

BUT DID IT ALSO SHRINK THE BUDGET? The couple volunteered for marriage counseling.

THE SOUND OF MUSIC: They hired a DJ and requested songs more on the "dance side, but not just circuit-party stuff." The unplanned first dance ("we thought it would be cheesy," says Jeff) was the Lighthouse Family's "High." The couple asked everyone to join them on the dance floor.

GEORGIA ON THEIR MINDS: Since southern tradition dictates that brides have white cakes, the couple opted instead for five types of chocolate cake with five different types of fruit on top (traditionally, the southern groom's cake).

WHO'S ON TOP? The couple tossed their boutonnieres into the crowd. "The single gay men were crawling over each other to get to them," Jeff says.

SOBERING THOUGHT: The photographer was intoxicated and the pictures came out awful. Luckily, they'd passed out disposable cameras to friends, which resulted in much better photos.

KEEPING THEIR RELIGION: Since both Michael and Jeffrey are Methodists—a denomination that refuses to perform same-sex ceremonies—they got in touch with the gay-founded Covenant Church.

LOSING YOUR LOVED ONES: Michael's mother and father refused to attend. "It's one thing to have a gay son," says Michael, "it's another to accept the fact that he's in love and getting married to another man."

HOTLANTA: The rehearsal dinner was held at Mary Mac's Tea Room, where Jimmy Carter dines on a regular basis.

HONEYMOON G-SPOT: A few days in Barcelona, then a couple more days in Sitges, a "mecca for gay vacationers in Europe."

PARTING WORDS: "We're in this together. It's not just about being straight or conservative; we wanted to make a commitment before God."

*Y*ou've decided to wed, your friends have given their blessings, and you're a blushing bride/groom. What next?

Before you dream of saying "I do" in the castle where Madonna married Guy, or having the biggest gay bash since Liza and David, you've got to figure out your budget. Most likely, you're in a different predicament from heterosexual couples, because you're footing the bill yourselves. Even if that's not the case and Mom and Dad are pitching in, it will probably be a set amount, not a blank check.

Pick a time, grab a pen or click a mouse, and figure out together exactly how much you can afford to spend. Remember, there isn't one planning step in the pages to come that can be addressed without knowing your budget. From sites and sounds to food and flowers, it all depends on how much money you can and want to spend. In order to move to the music, you've got to go with the cash flow.

Do not, under any circumstances, go into debt to pay for your wedding. The last thing you want is to start your new life together with a stack of bills bigger than your stack of thank-you notes.

While the average budget for American weddings is estimated at around twenty thousand dollars in the Midwest—and prices can increase by a third in

BALANCING
THE BUDGET

major cities—you can have an ideal wedding for half that figure or a beautiful ceremony for twice as much. Money doesn't buy happiness, and it doesn't buy the perfect wedding. Keep in mind what's important to you. A twelve-piece swing band a priority? Cut back on the expensive French wines. A massive guest list float your boat? Nix the five-course dinner and opt for a brunch instead. Whatever you decide, don't fall into the *I Love Lucy* trap and try to top your own Carolyn Appleby. What's crucial to your girlfriend's wedding may have absolutely no significance to you, so be sure you prioritize together when forming your budget.

Expense Report

Below is a list of traditional wedding-expense categories, not including honeymoon costs (which have too broad a range to list here). While these specifics can help you plan, you should know that many of them may not apply to you. Traditional-ceremony events like a rehearsal dinner are often avoided by gay couples, who'd rather find their own unique ways to celebrate their union. In other words, what Mom and Dad's generation felt compelled to plan for their weddings—bridal shower, a bachelor party—may not interest you in the least. Men have the advantage here (well, most men), in that they won't be buying expensive gowns. If two women means two gowns, either accept it and hold the reception at the YWCA, or bite the budget bullet and opt for Kmart instead of couture. Also, as mentioned above, prices vary from city to city; having a reception at the Plaza, à la Michael Douglas and Catherine Zeta-Jones, is obviously going to cost quite a bit more than throwing your bash at Howard Johnson's.

Once you've gone through these categories, pick and choose which ones apply to you, which ones you can discard altogether, and which ones you'll want to allocate more money to (you've always imagined the whole wedding party arriving in limos), as well as less (your cousin Luke is a professional photographer—he'll shoot the whole affair for the cost of film and a slice of cake).

A final word to help you with the initial budget: Reception and site costs (including food and liquor) normally account for about 45 percent of your budget. Photography can total another 10 percent. Flowers, attire (keep in mind we're talking *wedding dress* here; if you're wearing suits or simple dresses, the cost will be much lower), and music can each add up to 5 percent. Going by these—very general—statistics, you've got 30 percent of your budget left to spend on everything else below, and that's not including the honeymoon or such big-ticket extras as a wedding consultant. Knowing these percentages can help, especially when you realize that nabbing that Gothic mansion you want means you've got 4 percent of your budget left for everything else. Grab a pencil and use the blank spaces below to mix and match up your wedding costs. You can juggle costs to work around your specific budget. Who knows? You might even have fun.

The following are estimates, to help you get an idea of what you can spend. In chapter 6, you can check off more accurate prices for each item as you locate your vendors. However, you should get started with a rough cost estimate.

BUDGET BONUSES

Though not as common, and never required, here are some variables that you might want to consider when planning your ceremony:

- *Helping out with attendants' outfits.* Traditional etiquette dictates that members of the wedding party pay for their own attire, but nothing says "thanks for all your support" more than picking up (at least part of) the tab for attendants' clothing. If you're really rich in love, or just really rich, you could also help pay hotel costs for wedding-party members.
- *After-wedding brunch.* Since guests are often coming in from all over the world, a nice way to say good-bye is with a day-after brunch, which can be as informal as bagels and coffee at the local diner. It's also a great way to catch up with friends you didn't have much time to talk to the night before. Bonus: After-wedding events are also where everyone gets the gossip on who got plastered and stripteased to Christina Aguilera's "Dirrty," and who went home with the hottie bartender.
- *Goodie bags in hotel rooms.* Admit it, everyone's a sucker for a gift bag,

TRADITIONAL EXPENSES

Ceremony and Reception Site(s)
- ❑ Church or synagogue $_____
- ❑ Home $_____
- ❑ Banquet hall $_____
- ❑ Restaurant $_____
- ❑ Other (beach, boat, etc.) _____ $_____

Food
- ❑ Breakfast or seated brunch $_____
- ❑ Cocktail reception $_____
- ❑ Catered dinner $_____
- ❑ Cocktail hour followed by catered dinner $_____

Drink
Champagne toast as well as . . .
- ❑ Wine and beer $_____
- ❑ Limited open bar, then wine and beer at dinner $_____
- ❑ Open bar for entire reception $_____
- ❑ Top-shelf open bar for entire reception $_____

Flowers
- ❑ Bouquets and/or boutonnieres $_____
- ❑ Floral centerpieces $_____
- ❑ Elaborate floral displays at reception site $_____
- ❑ Flowers at ceremony and reception sites $_____

Photography/Videography
- ❑ Reliable friend who's an experienced photographer $_____
- ❑ Photographer for ceremony and reception $_____
- ❑ Photographer for ceremony and reception, color and black-and-white shots $_____
- ❑ Photographer and videographer for ceremony and reception $_____

Brides' Attire
- ❑ Two suits, off the rack $_____
- ❑ One suit, one dress $_____
- ❑ Two dresses, off the rack $_____
- ❑ Two custom-made wedding dresses $_____

Grooms' Attire
- ❑ Khakis and blazers $_____
- ❑ Two formal suits $_____

❑ Two rented tuxes $_____

❑ Top hats and tails $_____

Music

❑ Soloist or string quartet $_____

❑ DJ $_____

❑ Band $_____

❑ DJ and band $_____

❑ Other _____ $_____

Gifts

❑ Gifts to each other $_____

❑ Gifts to every member of the wedding party $_____

❑ Gifts to parents $_____

❑ Favors $_____

Rings

❑ Wedding bands $_____

❑ Diamond wedding bands $_____

❑ Engagement rings and wedding bands $_____

❑ Custom-designed wedding bands $_____

Transportation

❑ Car rentals $_____

❑ One limousine $_____

❑ Two limousines (one for the wedding party) $_____

❑ Rented getaway car $_____

❑ Other _____ $_____

Invitations/Stationery

❑ Homemade $_____

❑ Ready-to-buy $_____

❑ Custom-designed $_____

❑ Thank-you cards $_____

Rehearsal Dinner

❑ Lunch or dinner at home $_____

❑ Catered affair at home $_____

❑ Private party at bar $_____

❑ Seated dinner at restaurant $_____

Marriage License Fee

N/A, but we're keeping our fingers crossed.

which can contain items ranging from Starbucks gift certificates to lists of activities in the area. Don't blow your budget on this thoughtful gesture, though. It's simply a great way of reminding guests how much you appreciate their support.

Saving Grace

There's an old saying in the bridal business that if you want to cut your wedding costs in half, invite half as many people. Simplistic, yes, but there's a method to that madness. (And one of the first rules to budgeting is to nix ten guests from your list.) When you realize what's really important to you, as opposed to what society tells you is necessary—and, let's face it, you're not exactly wedding poster children—you'll quickly realize how many ways there are to save. Here are some cost cutters that won't dip into the fun fund. Once you read these over, you should be able to go back over your budget list and realize you've found more ways to save.

AND SPEAKING OF GUESTS . . .

One of the advantages to a gay wedding is that you're probably footing all, or most of, the bill. And that means you don't need to invite your dad's golf buddy's cousin twice removed. Gay weddings, on average, are about twice as small as their heterosexual counterparts. Since one person can easily add one hundred dollars to your budget, if you've got a hundred guests instead of two hundred, you've just saved ten grand. Isn't gay math wonderful?

OVERFILL

There's no rule saying guests have to leave your ceremony feeling like they've just had Thanksgiving dinner. There's also no rule that says your caterer has to have restaurants in Vegas or New York. Food's a big budget buster, so if it's not your top priority, turn a five-course meal into a brunch, or go with salmon instead of filet mignon. Food is not that much different from any other element of your wedding: You want to make it great, but you don't want to go over budget. Remember that great road trip you took when you camped on the beach, pigged out on fries at the local burger joint, and ended up skipping your final destination altogether because the scenery on the way was so wonderful? We're not suggesting a McWedding, but if you keep in mind what the day really signifies, as opposed to worrying about the status of what you're serving, then cutting down on dining costs can be food for thought.

SKIP THE FAVORS

They're nice, yes, but necessary, no. Remember, you've just given your guests food and drink, and probably a band, some dancing, and a chance to party with close friends and family. They don't necessarily need another sign of your affection when they leave. Keep in mind, too, that many guests will want to take home cake (which is a nice enough memento). Personalized matchbooks? It's completely up to you. Only allocate money that you can afford. Ditto disposable cameras—remember, guests bring their own.

MONDAY, MONDAY . . . OR TUESDAY OR SUNDAY

Friday and Saturday nights are the most common times of the week for places to book up, as well as the most expensive. So if you love that banquet hall, but hate the price, see if you can book it for another day of the week—or consider an afternoon ceremony. Another bonus about weeknight affairs is that guests don't drink as much—most will have to work the next day. As soon as you find a place, ask about alternate days and times; they won't think you're cheap, just smart.

IT'S THE TIME OF THE SEASON

By all accounts, June is still the most popular month to get married for heterosexual couples. Once again, save bucks by planning a less popular month such as February or October. You could even find that some friends will be relieved that your wedding's in November; they might have already been to five weddings over the summer. Another bonus: You'll have a better chance of booking the site of your dreams if you pick a date besides December 25.

MAKE YOURS A GIFT OF LOVE

You're about to make a lifelong commitment to each other. Isn't that enough of a gift for one day? While giving attendants thank-you gifts (they've put a lot into your wedding) is good sense, giving each other presents is completely optional. And remember, you've still got birthdays and all those other holidays to show your love.

TAME YOUR POISON

A champagne toast is pretty much de rigueur at all but a dry wedding, but other than that, you don't have to go cocktail crazy. Many couples serve only wine and beer with the meal, while others keep the bar time to a limit—usually while hors d'oeuvres are served. Another option is just a champagne toast along with a signature drink—the Mike and Tony Dirty Martini—to keep alcohol options limited. And if guests don't drink a lot, pay by the bottle or glass, not the time. Finally, ask your caterer or site manager about buying liquor yourselves, which can save a bundle. Do, however, expect to pay a corkage fee.

BLOOM IN LOVE

Tulips in January? Fine, if you don't mind importing them from someplace far away from your Aspen soiree. Think smart and buy flowers in season—your florist knows which blooms are the best buy for your wedding, so go through the list with him or her. And—the ultimate shocker—size really doesn't matter! (At least not at a wedding.) A simple red rose as a centerpiece can outdo a thousand white orchids. Sites can help, too: If you're marrying around Christmas, for instance, your space might already have beautiful arrangements. You can also cut down by concentrating more on beautiful plants than actual flowers.

DINNER DECISIONS

One of the most confusing names in wedding lore, the "rehearsal dinner" can actually be lunch, brunch, or a couple of lanes at the nearest bowling alley. You can also avoid it altogether. Regardless, don't feel that you have to break the bank and rent out the private room at the hottest new restaurant in town. Have a barbecue at your home or a friend's, or make it a cocktail hour instead, serving only hors d'oeuvres. Whatever you decide, fill guests in on the "food quotient" so they'll know how much to eat or not eat before the event.

LOVE AT SAME SITE

It doesn't take a rocket scientist to know you'll save money if the ceremony and reception are held at the same location. If that sounds uninspired (for others, it will be control-freak heaven), remember that many places have separate areas for vows and voguing. Even couples who have weddings at home often have the ceremony indoors, followed by an outdoor reception. Remember, too, that you won't have to worry about guests getting lost on their way to the reception or excess time between events.

Traditionally, Who Pays for What: A Heterosexual Primer

Wouldn't it be nice if you just said, "Dad, here's the date. Now where's your credit card?" Well, unless it's a sugar daddy you're talking to, that's unlikely to be the case at your wedding. But a planner wouldn't be a planner if it didn't give you the "traditional" money breakdown. Use this knowledge if your side of the family is paying for a significant chunk of the ceremony, but your partner's side wants to pitch in somewhere. Now you can give them some ideas of appropriate places. Also, if you and your honey are paying for the whole thing yourselves, but at the last minute Aunt Joan offers a gift of cash, you've got several good etiquette options you can throw at her—and hey, some of them even mean she'll get her name in print.

In days of yore (you know, before they published gay wedding books), the bride's family—not the bride—paid for the entire wedding, including, of course, that fabulous dress and all those flower arrangements. The lucky groom's mom and dad (or the groom himself) footed the bill for the rehearsal dinner, his and his parents' attire, the bouquet, and the honeymoon. (Now it's clear why men remarry more often than women: Their parents don't have to spend nearly as much money on the weddings, and the guys get to pick out lots of groovy travel options.) After the first engagement party, paid for by the bride's family, events were paid for by whoever hosted—namely, the groom's family or members of the wedding party (it's considered tacky for a relative of a bride to throw a shower). The bride's wedding band, of course, was paid for by her fiancé.

Today, even among heterosexuals, much of the above is folklore, and you don't have to look far to find a married couple who footed the bill for everything themselves. And just like straight couples, you buy each other rings, or purchase them together. About the only traditional financial given is that relatives still don't pay for showers (though it's certainly fine for them to help in the planning) and, perhaps out of superstition, brides, or their families, tend to pay for their own dresses. Other prewedding parties, however, such as an engagement bash or bachelor/bachelorette parties, can be thrown by anyone kind enough and gracious enough to offer themselves as hosts (and here's where their name gets on an invite). Everyone offering? There's no rule as to how many parties you can have. Just make sure that someone takes care of the stripper's fee ahead of time—there's a limit to how many bills will fill a G-string.

Dollars and Sense

Get used to it: You're about to sign on a lot of dotted lines. And even though this is a joyous occasion, whenever money's involved, you can't let the bubbly get the better of your brain. First, make sure you get everything in writing. No matter how much the florist flirts, never let him get away with "Don't worry, it'll be taken care of." If it's not on paper, it's not a done deal. Save all of your receipts; it's advisable to store them all in the same file. Whenever you read over any contract, if you don't understand, ask! If you still don't understand, ask again! Vendors will respect you for having lots of questions and getting straight down to business. Make sure every contract is signed and counter-signed, and always go over how much money you need to pay up front, what the cancellation policy is, and what happens if, say, the limo that was supposed to pick you up has a flat. It's also good to pay with a credit card whenever possible—often your only recourse if there's a major snafu. A bonus: Use a card that gives you frequent-flier miles and you could end up financing your honeymoon flight.

A Consultation on Consultants

The fact that your best friend Billy has seen *The Wedding Planner* seventeen times isn't reason enough to hire him as a consultant. The fact that Billy's the only one who's got the ambition to plan your wedding might be. Consultants can cost a whopping 10 to 15 percent of your budget, which is probably why it's usually people like J.Lo who most often hire them. There are, however, several good reasons to consider their services, especially if (a) you simply aren't genetically made to handle wedding details yourselves; (b) you're one of those people who always needs someone to reassure you (if you can't clothes shop alone, this may apply to you); or (c) you're planning your bash in a month or are going to be away for much of the time preceding your affair. Planners find everything you want: the site, the florist, the photographer, all within your budget. They will also look for ways for you to save money. A really good consultant will even step in to deal with problems between you and Mom, you and your fiancé(e), or you and your fiancé(e)'s mom.

Traditionally, there are two ways to go. There's a "full-time" consultant, who works on your wedding from start to finish. And there's the "daytime" planner, who comes in to arrange all the last-minute affairs you simply don't have time or nerves to take care of.

To find a consultant, ask friends for referrals (a tip to remember for every vendor you hire) or contact the American Association of Bridal Consultants (bridalassn.com) or June Wedding, Inc. (junewedding.com), which has an outstanding reputation as a gay-friendly organization. You can also look in the yellow pages under Party Planners or Wedding Consultants.

How to Make Sure That "Gay" Means "Happy"

These days, whether you're looking for a fabulous wedding consultant or some far-out formalwear, you shouldn't face too many obstacles when you tell vendors it's a same-sex wedding. If you're uncomfortable cold-calling, however, simply Google "Gay Weddings" to find a host of happy-homosexual vendors in your area. Several sites, like gayweddings.com, give you tips on both planning the wedding and where to honeymoon. Two things to remember: First, just because a site is labeled "gay-friendly" doesn't mean it's good. Second, you'll find a lot of "gay" sources on "gay" sites—meaning, everything from where to find rainbow wedding bands to female ministers who double as Elvis impersonators. Not that there's anything wrong with that! But just because you're gay doesn't mean you have to go that way.

Remember, if you come across any vendor, gay or straight, who's uncomfortable with your situation, or who in any way makes you feel uncomfortable, hang up that phone or delete that e-mail. There are plenty of other people in this world who'll be thrilled to take your money.

Here are a few gay websites we found useful for planning and partying:

www.pridebride.com
www.twogrooms.com
www.rainbowweddingnetwork.com
www.purpleunions.com
www.unionoflove.com
www.commitment-ceremonies.com

- *Cash bar.* No one's saying you need top-shelf liquor and a signature drink, but a cash bar is a nuptial no! Think of it this way—if you were throwing a dinner party, would you charge guests for the wine? And if you did, would they ever return?

- *No food or drink.* There are two things everyone expects at a wedding (besides a couple saying "I do"): something to drink and something to eat. If you decide that guests are going to get so liquored up they won't notice there are no snacks, you'll risk insulting both the nondrinkers and the guests who deliberately avoided dinner because they wanted to leave room for a meal. You don't want your friends' last memory of your wedding to be that pit stop they made to Burger King on the way home.

- *Letting guests tip.* They bought you a gift, they flew in from Peoria, they . . . have to leave a tip for the coat-check guy, the parking attendant, and the bartenders? Nope. Make sure tips are paid for before guests arrive. If you're afraid guests won't know what the deal is, leave a sign in a very visible area—near restrooms, for example—saying that all gratuities have been taken care of. And don't fret: A reputable bartender will know not to accept a little something extra for that mojito, no matter how cute your cousin Shelley tells her she is.

- *Inviting guests to the ceremony only.* Oh, sure, they get to hear your brother Ace read a personalized poem to the two of you, but they don't get to have champagne and cake afterward. No one's knocking the ceremony, but it's just plain bad sense to leave some guests out of the reception (truly meant as a party for everyone) so the two of you can save some dough. If you're overbudget, cancel the bubble machine instead.

- *Snapshot decisions.* We don't care how good your nephew Leroy is with a digital camera, it's your wedding, and these will be your photographs for the rest of your life. A friend who's actually a professional photographer is a great way to save money, but don't go with amateurs. Even if they have a knack for photography, they'll probably want to have fun at the wedding (in other words, *drink and party*), and you don't want to have to cut off the photographers' bar requests so that they don't accidentally cut off everyone's heads.

- *A name-brand wedding.* Yep: Some couples make deals with companies to advertise their products. But unless you want your centerpieces to say COURTESY OF 555-BUDWISE, this commercial venture is not recommended. It's your wedding, not a promotional video.
- *Plastic.* While plastic glasses are cheap and disposable, they're also, well, cheap and disposable. Unless you're having your ceremony outdoors or in an area where glass could be a hazard, save the partyware for your Super Bowl bash.

HOW TO BASH YOUR BUDGET—BUT NOT YOUR BASH

1. **Print ceremony and reception sites on the same invite.** It's not tacky, and those friends who can never keep track of where they put anything will thank you for it.

2. **Nonfloral centerpieces.** Nowadays, many couples are opting for such "alternative" table decorations as votive candles, vegetable and fruit displays, even shells. Really talented people are making their own. (You might want to check out a couple of how-to books before you opt to create Taj Mahal replicas out of apricot pits.)

3. **Vive la Napa.** Sparkling wine is often a cheaper alternative to French champagne. If anyone notices, pour them another.

4. **Let them eat cake.** Skip the dessert course and let them concentrate on your cake. (All the gym bunnies will be going carb-free anyway; others will be too full for both.)

5. **Allow nature to take its course.** Have your ceremony in an already beautiful site, like the beach or the park.

6. **Last rites.** Try this lifesaving travel option: Call funeral homes to rent limos. They usually don't need their vehicles at night.

7. **Mixed tape, dude.** It's so '70s and so okay. If you're having your ceremony in a more casual setting—like your home—burn a CD or create a mixed tape. That way you'll know all your requests are heard.

8. **Armed with Salvation.** Vintage dresses never go out of style, and they're never wrong for a wedding. The only added expense will be alterations.

9. **Practice penmanship.** Even in this computer age, handwritten envelopes can be winningly designed; just nix the caffeine intake before pen hits paper.

10. **Band of gold?** Diamonds may be a girl's—or girlfriend's—best friend, but you don't have to be able to cut glass to show class. Hold off on the expensive rings until a later date.

11. **Driver's education.** Show up in an old beat-up Chevy. Your friends will ooh and aah at the "antique" car you rented, when in reality it's just your dad's, well, old beat-up Chevy.

12. **Table for ten?** Seat more people at each table. You'll save on centerpiece costs, and possibly waiter service.

13. **Something borrowed?** It's not just for dresses anymore. Scour Grandpa and Grandma's storage for vintage jewelry, cuff links, or anything else that grabs you.

14. **Petal pushing.** Bring your ceremony flowers to the reception site, and use them either as centerpieces or to decorate the space. You can cut your flower costs almost in half while your guests will think they're seeing double.

15. **Smart shopping.** Once you pick your color scheme, wait till after a major holiday like Christmas or Valentine's Day to shop for candles. If you want candy as favors, wait till after the Halloween rush to purchase your own sugar variety.

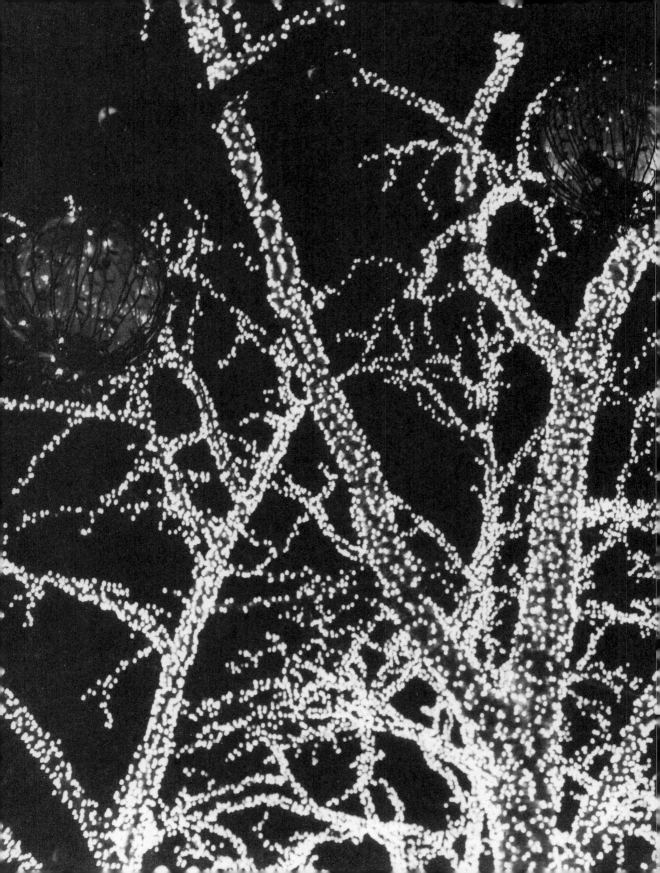

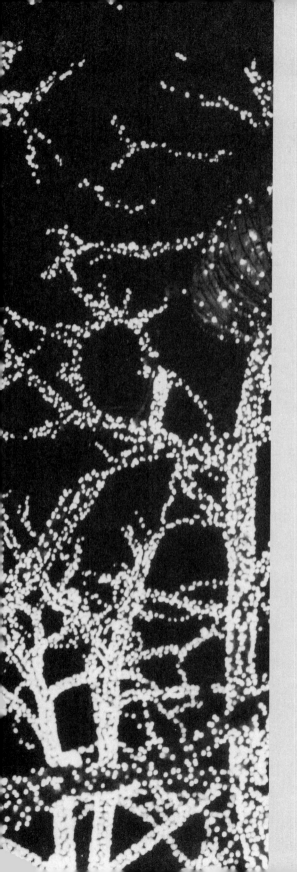

THE
STYLE
COUNCIL

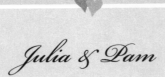

Julia & Pam

WHO: Julia Draper, thirty, and Pamela Jones, forty-four.

WHEN: Saturday, September 5, 1997.

WHERE: A friend's estate in Woodland Park, Colorado. The ceremony was held on a nearby hill overlooking Pikes Peak. Eighteen guests witnessed (only ATVs could make the trek), while sixty loved ones attended the afternoon reception on the estate's wraparound balcony.

FOOD, GLORIOUS FOOD: From three in the afternoon till eleven at night, guests chowed on a buffet of curried chicken, smoked salmon, and ribs.

ELEMENTS OF STYLE: Pam made both outfits, a simple skirt and blouse for her, and a pantsuit for Julia.

NOTICEABLY ABSENT: Alcohol (Pam and Julia are both in recovery).

NATIVE CUSTOMS: The ceremony was officiated by Sequoia Trueblood, a Native American elder, who blessed the couple with a peace pipe ceremony that extended the celebrations to two hours. (Pam and Julia are still recovering from the tobacco.)

COME TOGETHER: A DJ played an eclectic mix of songs, from pop to Motown. Patti LaBelle's "My Love, Sweet Love" was the couple's first dance, prompting Pam to get up and do the Money Dance. Julia was too busy eating to notice.

THAT'S WHAT FRIENDS ARE FOR: The DJ volunteered her services, the food was donated, and guests contributed money for the couple's honeymoon.

THE RING CYCLE: Two gold bands with inlaid diamonds. Both are weight lifters and wanted jewelry that was "functional and rugged."

MAKEOVER TIPS: "If we did it all over again, I would have invited my family," says Julia. "I didn't know at the time how they would have dealt with it or if they would have supported us. I think they would have been okay."

WHAT THEY OVERCAME: They didn't invite the husband of a straight friend of theirs. "We only wanted people who we knew believed in us," Pam says. "She handled it very well and attended the ceremony alone."

HONEYMOON G-SPOT: Starting in San Francisco, they drove south, stopping in Big Sur, and winding things up in Los Angeles.

PARTING WORDS: "We have no regrets. It was a perfect day."

*R*ight now a few things are probably racing through your mind. You're thinking, *Who does this homo think he is, telling me I need tips on style? I'm already fabulous.* (Guys, relax, this isn't a makeover chapter.) Or maybe, *A style chapter? I've already got enough photos of Jackie O's wedding dress.* (Once again, guys, relax, this isn't a fashion chapter.) The women reading this are just thinking, *I don't need a man to tell me about style. I bought new shoes. Can we move on?*

The style of your wedding is your next big step because, after you've figured out your budget, everything takes off from there. Take some time together to go over the kind of wedding you really want, and you'll probably find that a million questions pop up—most of which you'd never thought about before. Do you want a big wedding? Band or DJ? What about having your ceremony on the beach wearing khakis or sandals? Or how about a wedding on a Caribbean beach wearing jams and flip-flops? Do you want everyone including your fourth-grade teacher there, or just the girls from your book club who introduced you? What about other traditional touches like attendants and a rehearsal dinner? Are gay people even allowed to throw bouquets and have bachelor parties, and if so do garter belts have to be pink?

Let me make this as easy as possible by breaking down different types of weddings, guest-list options, and what you'll need to know about different types of ceremonies. Remember, there are two of you involved here, so if one of you is set on a ballroom affair for three hundred, and the other would like to drive off to a country cottage for the weekend with ten of your closest friends, do the only thing logical . . . go on a cruise! Compromise is not only essential, but can also be fun. You might discover that that dream wedding you swore you'd never back down on really starts to sound bogus compared to what your partner suggests. The wonder of being a couple in love comes into play here, as you realize again and again how much you learn from just listening to each other's fairy-tale fantasies.

When Size Matters

First, a head-count primer. Size and style go hand in hand, because if you want two hundred people at your wedding, you're not going to be able to hold it at that quaint new restaurant that you both adore. Similarly, if you're set on celebrating in a formal ballroom, keep in mind that it probably requires a minimum number of guests for you to reserve the space. After all, the site will most likely be supplying the food and drink.

So what comes first, the chicken or how many guests you'll need to serve it to? The answer to that philosophical question is entirely up to you. To help, here's a breakdown of whom you might want to invite, whom you should expect to invite, and whom you can leave out altogether—plus, pros and cons for each type of wedding.

WE ARE FAMILY

If you really want to have a small, intimate gathering, by all means, feel free. Make a list of those whose presence at your wedding would mean the world to you. A lot of times, that means a group of friends who've supported your partnership since day one, and who stood by you when others dismissed you as a "faux" couple whose wedding wasn't real. Whether or not your and/or your partner's parents accept your union will most likely determine if they're invited.

Usually, with this kind of affair, couples opt not to have a traditional wedding party (best man, flower girls), so you can stop worrying about a list of guys and girls you might otherwise feel obliged to invite—unsupportive sisters and brothers and relatives and their children. A great idea is for each spouse to have one attendant, usually a best friend, though the title *maid of honor* or *best man* is often discarded. When it comes to the invites, treat an informal ceremony and reception the way you would a dinner party—sit down and decide whom you'd really love to spend an evening with, eating, drinking, and celebrating your lives together.

Where problems can occur is with the uninvited. Once word is out that your brother Jake has been asked to attend because he was the one who encouraged the two of you to move in together, your uninvited brother, Jude, might feel slighted, even though he was rather indifferent to your union, or completely against it. Now's when you have to decide whether a wedding is a time to mend fences or to embrace only the people whom you know support your relationship. No one can make that decision except the two of you. The only invite rule—which applies to any guest list—is that there *is* no invite rule. (It's not just for homos anymore—heterosexual couples are now realizing that, when it comes to a wedding, no one but the ones getting married should, ultimately, decide who gets to come.)

PRO: You'll know that everyone at your ceremony is there because of their unconditional support for you and your partner.

CON: Ten years from now, as you watch the video, you might feel a pang of regret for not inviting your sister Jean, with whom you've since patched things up and in whose company you never mention your wedding.

SIZING UP

You've thought about it, and you just can't imagine your big day without dear Aunt Martha and those friends you still get holiday cards from. Now you're getting into that fifty-plus-sized wedding, where the expense and confusion can also rise. Once the list grows, you're going to have to worry about making sure out-of-towners have a place to stay. You'll also have to think about seating charts, and trying to find a time to wed when almost everyone can attend. A word of caution: Once your guest list hits this higher mark, think twice before scheduling your ceremony over a major holiday, religious or otherwise. Whereas your close friends will probably be thrilled to take off Memorial Day weekend to attend your wedding, it might not sit as well with Aunt Becky, who normally spends that weekend with her Long Island bridge club. Common for midsized weddings is to have attendants, and to even—gasp!—refer to them as maids of honor or best men. You can relax, however: You're not quite at the point, size-wise, where you need to figure out flower girls, ring bearers, and bubble attendants. Those are wedding-party members usually reserved for larger weddings. You're not going to be expected to have guests bring along the children.

As with planning any good-sized party, you'll inevitably encounter unexpected-guest issues when you work on the invite list. Suddenly, it will occur to you that if you ask the guys from your last Fire Island share, the ones from the previous summer are going to hear about it and, well, forget about getting invited to their next Fourth of July beach bash! Mom's going to call to say that if Aunt Melissa isn't invited, Aunt Selena will boycott out of loyalty. And just when you think you've got it all figured out, that co-worker who "always knew the two of you were going to get together" will start hinting that she'd like to do a mimed performance piece . . . with music.

The first thing to be prepared for is hurt feelings. It's inevitable and it's okay. Unless Mom and Dad are paying for a percentage of the wedding (and a sizable one at that), you can tell them that you just don't have the room for the friends or business associates they think should be invited. As for relatives, that's trickier because, well, word gets around and families gossip. You might find yourself playing diplomat for this size of wedding, and doing a lot of compromising. In other words, prepare to be addressing an envelope to a relative who's not exactly your favorite person in the world, but whom you're inviting to keep harmony all around. Ditto friends. Also, expect to compromise with your partner. It wouldn't be fair if you get to ask all the girls from your volleyball league, but your fiancée can't ask her acting-group buddies because one of them once had a crush on her. As for co-workers, same rule here as anywhere else. Ask everyone from your department, or just your supervisor. Don't, however, pick and choose. Office etiquette is tricky and, like it or not, important, even at your wedding. Chances are, too, that like any good host or hostess, there will be times when you're more concerned about hurting people's feelings than they are about getting their feelings hurt. Meaning, you might be devastated that the very first guy you came out to back in college can't be invited. He, on the other hand, might not even remember who you are—or which frat guy you were that night.

PRO: It's your wedding day! You want all those people who mean something to you to be there when you say your vows.

CON: Well, everyone except homophobic Uncle Bruce, who just happens to be married to Aunt Connie, the one who helped you prepare your coming-out speech to your parents.

THE BIGGER, THE BETTER

It's the bash of the century and you want everyone you've ever met to be there. And since (so far) you've never been invited to the Academy Awards, it's going to be equally as glamorous. This is the two-hundred-plus wedding. They're fun, fabulous, and a hell of a lot of work. There's a tendency for people to think that ceremonies such as these are reserved for heterosexual couples—and often because Mom and Dad insisted on it. Not true: More and more gay couples are throwing huge bashes because they feel like they've earned it. After coming out, facing homophobia, discrimination, meeting the man or woman of their dreams, and braving the storm by committing to each other in a country that hasn't embraced it, it's almost as much statement as it is celebration. Another factor: money. Since gay couples who wed tend to be older than their heterosexual counterparts (with jobs and savings to boot), they can afford to throw the party of the decade.

Big bashes almost always include traditional elements. From attendants to cake cuttings, from rehearsal dinners to postwedding brunches, it's frequently a weekend-long affair, with formal attire, natch. Religion often comes into play, with conservative ceremonies followed by blowout parties that last till dawn. And if someone's not invited, chances are they're not on your "gay-list."

The good news is, since you want everyone there, it's almost *easier* to come up with a guest list. An extravagant wedding like this usually means you'll pull out your address books and start writing down names. Then you work from there, inviting co-workers, relatives, even those high school buddies you've not been in constant contact with. Don't be surprised, however, that, even with such leeway, you still come up with more people than you'd originally thought of. It's a good rule of thumb with all party planning to anticipate about 25 percent more people than you initially think of—their names will surface in the months to come. Your biggest problem with this type of wedding is that, as soon as word goes around that it's a big affair, many guests will automatically assume they can bring a date *(unless the invite says they can, your guests are not expected to)*, while others will call you to tell you their kids will be tagging along (even though you stated "adults only" on the invites). You've taken on the role of party planner here; you're going to have to expect a few crashers. How to deal? Be firm: If Suzie Newbeau tells you she plans to bring the guy she met at Hooters last Friday night, tell her up front you don't have the room. Similarly, you'll have to inform Aunt Fertile that her seventeen children can't attend, but you'd be happy to look for a babysitter in your area, should she be traveling to the wedding. You're not being rude, and you don't have to lie. This is your day, and certain rules have to apply.

Don't even think about a party of this size if you have an aversion toward bachelor or bachelorette parties (someone's bound to throw one), or have an allergic reaction to the Macarena (someone's bound to request it). You have to relinquish control over certain elements of your bash once it gets this big. After everyone's had enough punch, the life of the party *becomes* the party.

PRO: You get to give so many people the time of their lives!
CON: Expect to say, "I've heard so much about you." A lot!

The Dating Game

You know your guest list and you're ready to roll. You've even compromised on that beloved belle epoque mansion that graced the cover of *Architectural Digest* a few months back. Time to call the caterer, right? Wrong. Before you can confirm where you're going to hold your ceremony, you've got to make sure the space is available. Since popular sites book up to a year in advance, make a date now! You'll be surprised how often it's not just your honey who's in demand that day.

Your smartest option here is, assuming you have chosen a site, to pick several possible dates before you make your calls. The space isn't available that Friday night? Is Saturday an option? And if that doesn't work, would you consider a weeknight or a brunch affair? Now is the time to think about different months. If the botanical gardens really bloom in April, see about a June date as a second choice. Assuming you take care of this within the first couple of months of planning, you shouldn't have too much trouble finding the place of your dreams on the day you desire.

Many couples, however, make the date the priority. It's common to wed on an anniversary, a holiday, or some other day that's special to the two of you—"We're night owls, so we insist on having our ceremony when daylight saving time begins." You're not alone if you're insistent on a particular day, but here again, you have to leave your site options open. In this scenario, scribble out ten different possibilities and call immediately. Keep in mind, too, that if your ceremony and reception sites are at different locales, you've got double the date dilemma. Also, if that special day does fall on February 14, face the cold hard facts now: You're going to have to spend more money to reserve it. Once again, we can't stress enough how important it is to take care of these details immediately.

Affairs of the Heart

Herewith, several ceremony options: what you need to know, what you need to do, and what unexpected surprises you might run into.

IT'S A FORMAL AFFAIR

So much for that cliché that gay people only want to be married naked in a hot tub with a transsexual-Ruth-Westheimer-impersonator-*cum*-minister and twelve bridesmaids dressed like cast members from *Mamma Mia!* (Besides, that wedding's *so* been done.) More and more couples are finding they want the traditional wedding (church included) that they grew up watching on TV and in the movies, that their parents had, and that their straight friends and co-workers had. Guys are registering at Tiffany and girls are going couture. These couples tend to have big guest lists with rehearsal dinners, receiving lines, engagement parties, showers, cake cutting, even bouquet and garter tosses and rice or birdseed at the finish. There will be blocks of hotel rooms reserved for out-of-town guests, and one hell of an extravagant honeymoon—how does two weeks in Europe sound?

WHAT YOU NEED TO KNOW: Traditionally, for a formal evening affair, the dress code for the groom and any ushers is black tie. For the bride, it's a long white gown with a train. For a daytime affair (before 6 P.M.), women can wear a shorter dress, and the men can wear suits and ties—gray strollers are the most popular option. There are usually several attendants, and their choice of clothing is dictated by you. Children are frequently not invited. As for food, like everything else, none of this is written in stone, but, chances are, if your friends are getting all gussied up, they're going to expect some good eats. Also, it's a nice touch to print or engrave formal invitations. You'll have to have sorted out any religious elements ahead of time (see chapter 2). Also, expect that many sites—restaurants, private homes, art galleries—will not only require you to work with their caterers or chefs, but also have many limitations. For instance, a restaurant might not have a dance floor, and there might be limits as to what type of music can be played. Art galleries have, well, art, so don't be surprised if red wine's forbidden, or that certain areas are off limits completely. Another thing to take note of: room size. Restaurants, especially, are notorious for having small private rooms for special events; you might need to scale down that guest list considerably. Dancing might have to be scratched off your list altogether.

WHAT YOU NEED TO DO: Ask what's available, and what you must provide. If your affair is being held in a historic home, the site might already be set up beautifully, meaning a minimum of floral designing is needed. On the downside, you might have to rent everything: Like that "living room" you had growing up, the furniture is meant to be adored, not actually used. If your wedding's being held at a site that offers a package deal, make sure to find out what that includes—and what it excludes. You might find that your banquet hall provides every possible amenity, including a chuppah that doubles as a garden walkway. It also might not allow for you to add any personal touches of your own, down to the centerpieces or that one-of-a-kind cake you wanted. A good rule of thumb: If the site you want is empty, you can pretty much rest assured it's your responsibility to fill it up. Likewise, if it's full, those tangerine-orange place mats are probably there to stay. Regardless, ask and you *might* receive.

THE UNEXPECTED: Reality can still bite, so know that the more formal the site, the more likely it is that someone's not going to be so thrilled that a gay wedding's being held there. If you do manage to land a swank country club because the owners are old family friends, or a university club because you're an alumnus, that doesn't mean the on-site caterer or even the waiters are happy about homos. Do yourself a favor and ask up front if anyone expects this to be a problem. Gay people, more than just about anyone, know the dangers of silence, so don't be quiet before your wedding. On a brighter note, we live at a time in which gay people have become accepted on a much broader scale. On that note, everyone at your wedding, one way or another, might feel pretty, and witty, and definitely gay.

MIDDLE OF THE ROAD

In a world where people are reluctant to dress up for a night on the town unless it includes box seats at the opera, think of the semiformal wedding as the equivalent of a Broadway matinee: People will dress appropriately, yet comfortably. Guests don't want to embarrass anyone by showing up in ripped jeans and a tank top (unless, of course, the wedding's in LA), but they also don't want to be pulling at that tie all night long, or reapplying Band-Aids every couple of hours so their too-tight rented shoes don't make their feet blister. Most likely, if you're contemplating this kind of ceremony, you're one of those people, too—and you probably avoid the opera on opening night. Probably the most common of all weddings, gay or straight, a semiformal affair gives you more leeway in wedding planning than a formal affair, because it's usually held in a spot that doesn't have rigid rules and regulations.

Granted, you can still hold your bash at a restaurant, and you can still walk down the aisle of a house of worship. Just like the clothes in your closet, different labels have different degrees of formality. Other options include loft spaces, banquet halls, and hotels. As for the wedding party and traditional touches, it's pretty much up to you. You're not being so formal that guests will expect a receiving line—though, in general, they're a great way for you to make sure you acknowledge everyone who came—while at the same time, you'll probably serve something a little more exciting than tuna casserole.

WHAT YOU NEED TO KNOW: In traditional hetero ceremonies, the bridal attire is less rigid, which means women can get away with a shorter dress and a different color than white. Men can wear tuxedos or dinner jackets for the evening; suits are fine for daytime. In general, there are no more than two attendants, and it's common to let them choose their own attire. Children are frequently invited. For semiformal affairs, it's often common to opt for a buffet meal instead of a sit-down dinner. Much of the preparation will probably be up to you. Places like banquet halls, hotel ballrooms, and loft spaces usually let you take charge of the wedding, letting you find the band or DJ, caterer, florist, and so forth. If you're having your ceremony in a popular spot, find out how many weddings or other events it's holding that day. You don't want to discover after it's too late that you have to be out by five o'clock to make way for another wedding. Similarly, you don't want your first-dance song drowned out because of the junior prom being held in the room across the hall.

WHAT YOU NEED TO DO: Tell people how to dress. Unlike the term *black tie,* which pretty much sums up the level of formality at a wedding, semiformal affairs often confuse guests, who don't know if they should wear a tux, a cocktail dress, or jeans and a dress shirt. Simply write "black tie optional" or "cocktail attire" on the invites to clue guests in on how they should dress. No one wants to stand out at your ceremony; your guests will be thrilled you've given them a guideline. If the affair is outdoors, be more lax with the dress code.

THE UNEXPECTED: Speaking of dress etiquette, don't be surprised if, despite your doings, someone in the wedding party shows up in alligator boots while everyone else is wearing rented black shoes. There's really nothing you can do, so laugh it off and think how funny it will look in the wedding video.

DRESS? PREFERRED.

You're allergic to ties or you haven't worn a skirt since your Girl Scout days. You and your partner are into barbecues, bong hits, and beer. You probably see your wedding as more of a party than a style statement—the significance of your vows having nothing to do with grandiose planning—and you certainly don't want it to resemble any of those stuffy "breeder" ceremonies you're periodically forced to attend. Many couples who opt for an informal ceremony do so because they are determined that the only way they will say "I do" is with a wedding that skips traditional elements altogether. No showers and no receiving line, and if there is a cake, chances are you won't be stuffing it into each other's mouths. For straight couples, the archetypal informal wedding would be a mad dash to Vegas. Gay couples have a whole new world in which to find their place.

WHAT YOU NEED TO KNOW: Informal basically means there are no rules for attire. Wear what you want, and discuss it with your partner. It's common not to have a wedding party, except for maybe a close friend to help the two of you and offer support. Children are often invited. No matter how hot you look in a Speedo, on your wedding day your significant other might prefer you opt for something a little more appropriate, like board shorts. Since informal weddings tend to be smaller, invitations are often handwritten. Now that we live in the Internet age, there's been much debate over the etiquette of e-mailing invites. Use your own judgment on this one, but many think that a wedding, no matter how subdued, is best announced via snail mail.

WHAT YOU NEED TO DO: Pick and choose. An informal wedding could be a picnic in the park; a day at the beach, city hall, or your favorite bar; or a gathering of close friends and relatives in your backyard. If you do still want to have the ceremony in a house of worship, keep in mind that your formality level will go way up—you can change into cutoff jeans and halter tops later. Just as with a semiformal ceremony, let guests know the dress code and any special precautions they'll need to take. For example, if you do have a beach ceremony, advise them to wear comfortable shoes. Stilettos are hell to maneuver on the sand . . . trust me!

THE UNEXPECTED: Go too informal, and guests might not take the wedding too seriously. Translation: They might not realize they have to call and cancel, or they might not bother with a gift. By either phone, word of mouth, or your invitations, let everyone know that your wedding is an extremely important day and you'd love to have them there to share the joy.

Having a Wonderful Time . . . Wish You Were Here

Before you book that hot-air balloon wedding, decide to say your vows on a ski slope in Vail, or swim down the aisle in a scuba-diving ceremony, think about the people you're inviting and how, if at all, accessible the location is to them. (Feel free, of course, to think about the people such a wedding allows you *not* to invite!) A winter ceremony in the mountains is a charming idea, but will Grandma Maria be comfortable at that altitude? A love-among-the-cacti service? Heatstroke hurts, and your sun-sensitive friends might have to skip it altogether. Even a glorious Caribbean wedding can be tainted by the fact that, in today's world, many people simply don't care about your wedding enough to get over their fear of flying. The fact is, anytime you decide to wed in an unusual location, you're going to alienate a certain number of guests. One way around the challenge is to have that initial roller-coaster service, then arrange a big party on solid ground in the near future. You can make your wedding even more accessible this way because, in addition to offering two distinct dates for people to choose from, if you have the second ceremony in the most neutral place of all—the city where you live or where you grew up—many guests who might not have been able to travel for your first wedding should be able to make it the second time around.

Alternative Alternative Wedding Sites, Pros and Cons

The good, the bad, and the utterly fabulous reasons to pick some less traditional sites.

BEACH

PRO: The ocean makes a beautiful backdrop, and the sounds of the waves are as harmonious as the two of you.

CON: Sand sucks. Advise guests to wear comfortable clothing—and no hose!

PARK

PRO: The sound of birds, the smell of grass . . .

CON: Mosquitoes and other bugs love it just as much as you do. Supply repellent, and make sure you're in a shady spot.

LOFT

PRO: So trendy and so downtown. Often with great city views.

CON: It's a blank canvas. You might have to rent everything, and there won't necessarily be a kitchen.

MUSEUM

PRO: Love among the Picassos. What a beautiful expression.

CON: Spilling wine on art will leave the owners blue. Expect strict regulations on food and drink.

CRUISE SHIP

PRO: Gay weddings at sea are becoming more popular. Honeymoon built in.

CON: Cruising's popular on cruise ships, too. Be wary of wayward glances, or the honeymoon might be over before it begins.

BOAT OR YACHT

PRO: The very idea screams *glamour*. Guests will be flattered just to be invited.

CON: Except the ones who get seasick. Also, make sure your caterer overstocks; you can't order more champagne once you've left the shore.

VINEYARD

PRO: Beautiful and sophisticated, and it's pretty easy to locate wine.
CON: Like the grapes, you'll most likely be required to use what's already on the property. And in such a pristine setting, DJs and wine simply don't mix.

BOTANICAL GARDENS

PRO: Time to mark "flowers" off your to-do list.
CON: Allergies. You or any guests might spend the day in tears—for the wrong reasons.

NUDIST COLONY

PRO: It's all about the soul.
CON: Do you really want to see Aunt Buffy's soul exposed?

There's No Place Like Home?

You're vowing to spend your lives together, so why not make those vows at the actual space you'll be spending your days? A home wedding has lots of advantages. First, you like the decor—and if you don't, put this book aside for a bit and start looking for new digs, or just a good decorator. Your friends will know how to get there (always a plus when it comes to last-minute stress). You can have any music you want, there are no restrictions on food or drink, and you don't have to worry about rushing through your vows so the next wedding can begin.

A couple of considerations to keep in mind: If you're having all or part of the ceremony outdoors, you'll need to rent a tent in case of rain. Caterers supply a wait staff, but you're going to have to provide the extra chairs, tables, and any other wedding necessities—and if you're inviting two hundred guests, that most likely means a portable toilet or two. Parking may be a problem: If it's a city wedding, let guests driving in know ahead of time where there's a garage. Suburban or country affair? Call the city council to see if there are any parking restrictions you need to be aware of (and just to give them a heads-up that you're having a wedding). To keep the peace whether it's town or country, it's never a bad idea to invite neighbors you're on good terms with. They'll be less likely to complain about Pink blaring from your CD player if they've been asked to help get the party started.

FIND YOUR WEDDING STYLE QUIZ

Still having trouble determining what kind of wedding you want? Take this quiz to get into the groove. (Only one answer per question, please.)

What's your idea of the perfect outdoor activity?
1. Opera in the park
2. A softball game or tennis
3. Trinket shopping at the flea market
4. Heading to an amusement park
5. Sex

Growing up, your favorite reading was:
1. Anything by Dickens
2. *The Catcher in the Rye*
3. Nancy Drew mysteries
4. *Mad* magazine
5. I didn't read, I lived!

What's your favorite holiday?
1. Christmas
2. Thanksgiving
3. Fourth of July
4. Halloween
5. February 29

Your perfect Saturday night consists of:
1. Dinner and a show
2. Drinks with friends
3. You and your TiVo
4. Coming home Sunday morning
5. A Ouija board and hot wax

When it comes to cooking, you:
1. Start preparing the day before
2. Tell the maître d' you'd like your usual table
3. Order in
4. Grab a slice of pizza on the run
5. Eat something you grew yourself

What's your favorite sexual position?
  1. You mean there's more than one?
  2. Whatever pleases your partner
  3. It's all good
  4. One that involves toys
  5. At thirty-five thousand feet

Choose your favorite gay icon (check either Male or Female, not both):
  (Male)
  1. Judy Garland
  2. Barbra Streisand
  3. Joni Mitchell
  4. "Material Girl" Madonna
  5. Agnes Moorehead

  (Female)
  1. Katharine Hepburn
  2. Jodie Foster
  3. Ellen DeGeneres
  4. "Ray of Light" Madonna
  5. Eleanor Roosevelt

The perfect date movie is:
  1. *Casablanca*
  2. *Annie Hall*
  3. *When Harry Met Sally . . .*
  4. *The Rocky Horror Picture Show*
  5. *The Exorcist*

If you could wear only one label, it would be:
  1. Giorgio Armani
  2. Donna Karan
  3. Gap
  4. Versace
  5. Jaclyn Smith for Kmart Collection

Which *Sex and the City* character do you relate to most?
  1. Charlotte
  2. Carrie

3. Miranda
   4. Samantha
   5. Mr. Big

What's your favorite sitcom?
   1. *M*A*S*H*
   2. *Cheers*
   3. *Roseanne*
   4. *Absolutely Fabulous*
   5. *The Addams Family*

Pick a favorite Mary:
   1. Queen of Scots
   2. Tyler Moore
   3. Martin
   4. J. Blige
   5. Bloody

What's your favorite cocktail?
   1. Martini
   2. Wine
   3. Rum-and-Coke
   4. Something that requires salt and a lemon wedge
   5. Antidepressants

Who would you most like to be interviewed by?
   1. Barbara Walters
   2. Mike Wallace
   3. Connie Chung
   4. David Letterman
   5. Robin Byrd

You'd most like to attend a party hosted by:
   1. Bankers
   2. Writers
   3. Teachers
   4. Actors
   5. Transvestites

WHERE YOU FIT IN

How to score: Give yourself one point for every answer corresponding to "1" and two points for every "2" answer, and so on.

If you scored 15 to 26 points:

You're a traditionalist. You'll most likely want a large, formal wedding with many of the customary features. Chances are you'll have your ceremony in a house of worship, followed by an elaborate reception. Plan on having lots of attendants, a seated meal, and a band and DJ (there will be dancing till dawn). Traditional dress will be the order of the day, and you might even go so far as involving children in the wedding. Lots of parties will be held before and after the big day. Don't rule out a long-weekend wedding, especially one that falls over a holiday. A great site would be a tent by the beach or in the country. You might consider a wedding consultant, because there will be so many details to attend to. Remember, you've got to think about favors, flowers that complement the linens, and exactly who stands where in the receiving line. A nice touch? A raw bar or a sundae station for the kids.

If you scored 27 to 38 points:

You're the intimate type. You'd like a large guest list, but you want to make sure you have ample time to spend with all who attend. Cocktail chatter is a must, so even if you go for a seated meal, make sure there's time for hors d'oeuvres. A restaurant reception might be the way to go—one where you're close, personal friends with the owner—so you can seat friends with people you'd love to introduce them to. Since DJs are rather loud and impersonal, opting for a small band or a jazz combo is a great substitute. You don't want a large wedding party, but it might be nice to have a couple of attendants. Unless you know they're going to be well behaved, leave the children to babysitters. Forgo the bouquet and garter toss, as well as any bachelor/bachelorette parties beforehand. A rehearsal dinner with your closest friends the day before works just as well. A nice touch? A martini bar/lounge area.

If you scored 39 to 50 points:

Your style is casual. It's a wedding, not a White House dinner. That guest list will include the people who are important to you—if they want to bring a date, that's cool. Ditto the kids. Since you certainly don't want to feel like a stuffed shirt, or be wearing one, the attire will be comfortable and cazh, and you'll insist that guests dress the same. Don't make the invite list too large—more people means extra preparation. If you have attendants, they'll pick out their own outfits. Writing your own vows is a must. Reception options might include your home or a banquet hall, though you shouldn't rule out a park or beach, provided the restrictions are minimal. As for food, how does buffet sound? You're going to be a whiz at saving money—cutting costs is much more important to you than, say, the perfect site. A nice touch? Planning a day-after event with the people who traveled all that way to be at your wedding.

If you scored 51 to 62 points:

You're a party animal. You've taken a big step in having a wedding, and it's going to be a night to remember (that is, if you can actually remember anything). The only require-ment for location is no rules! The last thing you want is a midnight wedding curfew, or complaints about too much noise. Your medium-sized guest list is only going to include people who expect the unexpected. Chances are, your friends won't *want* to bring the children. The food will be something fun and different—how does Middle Eastern or Mexican sound? Your attire will no doubt be a fashion statement, or antistatement, and you'll tell the guests to dress the same way. Attendants? Forget about it! And if you can't find the perfect rock band, you're going to get the hottest DJ in town. Last call? Won't happen. The drinks will flow as long as the guests hold up. As for your wedding night, who needs immediate intimacy when your friends are with you? (Besides, you probably already snuck off somewhere for a honeymoon sneak preview.) A nice touch? Shot glasses as favors—shots included.

If you scored 63 to 75 points:

You're the outrageous type. Okay, so you've decided to commit. However, the last thing you're going to do is anything that reeks of tradition or formality. You'd love to have your ceremony on a mountain, in the woods, at the home of Donny *or* Marie. The guest list will be small; not everyone "gets you." And the first person who complains about the incense is out of there. Potluck would be a great food option, as your psy-chic makes a wicked sake-and-tofu stew. Instead of a band or DJ, you'll pick some-thing more meaningful to you, like a Tibetan monk chanter. Kids are always welcome; they are the most open-minded of anyone you know. You'd never rent a limo, but you'd certainly arrive via public transportation or a helicopter. As for gifts, why should you register when all you need is love? A nice touch? Wear underwear, at least for the ceremony.

Your Place in the Sun

Now that you've gotten a few ideas about how you want your wedding to go, it's time to take that plunge and start making some calls. You've figured out the guest count, you know the date, and you've set your sights on the perfect site. Here's a checklist to help you keep track of the plans you've made so far. Mark off categories as your dream ideas become reality.

Date _____

    Alternate date 1 _____

    Alternate date 2 _____

House of worship ceremony

    ❑ Yes

    ❑ No

Reception site (if not at a house of worship)

    Site 1 _____

    Site 2 _____

    Site 3 _____

Time

    ❑ Morning

    ❑ Afternoon

    ❑ Evening

Number of guests _____

Attendants

    ❑ Yes

    ❑ No

    If yes, how many _____

Formality

- ❏ Formal
- ❏ Semiformal
- ❏ Casual

Food

- ❏ Seated dinner
- ❏ Buffet dinner
- ❏ Brunch
- ❏ Breakfast
- ❏ Hors d'oeuvres

Dancing

- ❏ Yes
- ❏ No

Music

- ❏ Band
- ❏ DJ
- ❏ Both

Parties

- ❏ Shower
- ❏ Bachelor/bachelorette party
- ❏ Engagement party
- ❏ Rehearsal dinner
- ❏ Postwedding breakfast, lunch, dinner

THE
WEDDING
PARTY

Floyd & Marc

WHO: Floyd Sklaver, thirty-seven, and Marc Acito, forty-four, after a ten-year courtship.

WHEN: Wednesday, July 23, 2003.

WHERE: The Rose Garden of the British Columbia Legislator, Victoria, British Columbia. The couple eloped from Seattle and decided the Legislator was the most visible place to declare their love.

REALITY TV: Their marriage ended up being on national news that evening, as did a recording of their vows.

NOW THAT'S WHAT I CALL ROOM SERVICE: A waitress at the Emperor's Hotel, where the newlyweds stayed, served as a witness to the wedding.

ELEMENTS OF STYLE: Short sleeves and slacks were the garments of choice.

FUNNY GUYS: The couple broke into an impromptu version of "Sadie, Sadie" on the ferry to Canada.

HONEYMOON HOSPITALITY: They were upgraded to a suite at the hotel (with chocolates in their room) when they told the clerk they were getting married.

TRADITIONAL TOUCH: Something old ("us"), something new ("the rings"), something borrowed (a friend's garter tied around Marc's biceps), something blue (Floyd wore a blue shirt).

BEST MAN'S BEST FRIEND: Their dog did the duties.

MAKEOVER TIPS: "Had we thought about it a little longer, we could have brought a whole group of people with us. Our parents could have come," says Floyd.

LOOKING BACK TO THE FUTURE: "We won't have a ceremony in the States until it's legal," says Marc. "Then we'll have a huge party and tell everyone exactly what gifts we want."

WHAT THEY OVERCAME: The local newspaper wanted to put their wedding announcement in the "Commitment Ceremonies" section. Once they got back from Canada, they called the paper with the news, and the marriage announcement appeared in the "Weddings" section.

PARTING WORDS: "I never thought we'd live to see this day. We're really married," says Marc.

One of the joys of putting together a gay wedding is probably similar to one of the joys of putting together a book on gay weddings: You get to make a lot of your own rules. After all, who's going to judge you if your flower girl's a guy, if your bridesmaids wear matching fake tattoos instead of dresses, or if you're a vision in flaming red as you walk down the aisle—or just flaming? Bridal etiquette doesn't officially extend to same-sex ceremonies, so you and your partner are your own best judges. Until there's a law that says homosexual commitment is just as important as a straight union *(Beantown, can you hear me?)*, we wouldn't have it any other way.

That said, there's a reason why bridal magazines and books are so abundant. It's a big day and you want guidelines. Part of the planning involves your closest friends and family. As such, you want their participation to be both memorable and fun, and as stress-free as possible. You also don't want to offend anyone, especially if they canceled their week at the ashram to be with you.

Your wedding party can be large or small, or nonexistent. Whatever you decide, they'll no doubt play a large part in the ceremony—there will be fittings to worry about (even if you decide you'd like your attendants to pick their own outfits, they're going to want to look their best). You might want your female friends to help you decide what to wear, and both men and women can help with last-minute problems you simply don't have time to deal with. More and more, moms and dads participate in gay weddings; they might do readings, throw you a party, or simply walk you down the aisle. Most important, a member of the wedding can offer support during a time that can be extremely stressful. Remember, attendants are helping you out a great deal; make sure you don't overwork them, and always find a way to reward them.

Your Attendants, Please! Traditionally, Who Does What

In heterosexual-wedding lore the bride has an honor attendant called either a maid or matron of honor (the latter simply being a married woman), bridesmaids, possibly junior bridesmaids ("tweens," in modern lingo), and a flower girl. The most specific label you can give for the honor attendant is "right-hand gal." She helps pick out the dress, throws the bride a shower, and takes care of any last-minute emergencies that pop up. The honor attendant is usually a close friend, but there are no rules saying she can't be a mother or another close relative. Even at straight weddings, some women choose to have a man fill this duty (usually called a man of honor); the only difference is that he wears the same thing as the other men in the wedding party, and he's not expected to do anything that would "emasculate" him, like throw a bachelorette party or hire the stripper.

Bridesmaids can come in any number—two or ten, there's no set rule—they attend showers and are invited to all parties, and they're expected to help out in some capacity—rumor has it they even enjoy these tasks! Over the years bridesmaids have been poked fun at because the position requires a lot of time, no one's putting a ring on their finger, and for some strange, never-explained reason, the dresses they're required to wear would have made Milton Berle look like Miss America. A junior bridesmaid differs only in that her dress isn't as revealing as a bridesmaid's, and, since she's still rather young, she's probably not quite as bitter about the experience as her older "colleagues." A flower girl simply tosses petals down the path before the bride walks down the aisle.

On the male side, the best man shares pretty much the same responsibilities as the female honor attendant, though he's also expected to supply the rings, make the first toast, sign the marriage license, hold any cash needed (officiant, tips), get the tuxes back to the rental store on time, and make sure the bride and groom aren't so drunk or so in bed that they miss their honeymoon flight. Ushers (brothers, friends, future brothers-in-law's friends) pretty much do what the word implies. They seat people at the ceremony, making sure that all latecomers are taken care of, and stick around afterward to check that nothing's been left behind. Ushers are frequently the official "honeymoon car makeover artists," though that's by no means a requirement of the job.

RECEIVING ATTENTION

The wedding party also makes up the all-important receiving line. Not simply a formality, a receiving line is a great way to thank all the people for coming to your wedding, and it's often the only sure way you know you will have spoken with everyone in attendance. This is especially helpful if you are having a large affair. If you're holding your ceremony at a house of worship, it's usually easiest to form the line right outside as people are leaving. If there's no room at the site, or if the space is needed (your photos, another wedding), the line is formed at the reception. Traditionally, whoever hosts the wedding heads the line. In most cases that would be the mother and father of the bride, followed by the mother and father of the groom. Next come the bride and groom, her honor attendant, and the bridesmaids. Over the years the "rules" have changed, and it's become optional to have fathers and attendants in the line—they can mingle instead. This shortened version of the receiving line is also best when you have a large number of guests. Really savvy couples have been known to serve hors d'oeuvres and cocktails while guests wait in line to be greeted. This last option is not always affordable or possible, especially at a church or synagogue, unless passing around a flask and a bag of chips is your idea of a good pick-me-up.

And Now for Something Completely Different

Much of the etiquette listed above will come into play at your own wedding. As you get closer to your big day, however, you'll likely come up with a list of questions that have never entered the heterosexual-wedding vernacular.

Your fiancée's not involved enough in wedding planning. How do you tell her?

The days are past when this was only a problem involving men. Whereas most gay males seem to take a fairly equal interest in wedding planning (imagine that!), with two women, one of them often says, "Just tell me when to show up."

You've got two options here, both adopted from straight etiquette. Either you accept it (make sure you first ask yourself if you're being too demanding), or you assign her small tasks that she'll enjoy doing. She might take care of the registry, haggle with vendors, or plan the honeymoon, including looking for all the best deals, making the flight arrangements, and taking care of any precautions, such as making appointments to get vaccinations. She can also research guidebooks to find activities for both of you.

When two men have a wedding, is there a father–son dance?

Even if your dad is completely accepting of your sexuality and ceremony, there's a very good chance he'll feel awkward taking a spin around the dance floor with you and your partner. Is getting him good and drunk the answer? Nah, that way he'll probably end up kissing an usher or fulfilling his secret *Full Monty* ambitions. After the first dance, the order of dances is one of the wedding traditions that same-sex couples most often question. If you simply eliminated a father–son round, would it be fair to have a mother–son dance? That seems awkward and sends a message (no matter how untrue) that Dad's uncomfortable with the ceremony.

Like so many wedding rituals, this is definitely one that many gay couples decide needs to be reexamined. The solution? Either eliminate all dances, or have a first dance between the two of you and then invite everyone up on the floor to get down together.

Two women are having a ceremony, and both are extremely close to their parents. Which family pays?

We've heard stories that whichever woman wears the most conventional attire should be the one to ask Dad for cash. While there's nothing wrong with that idea, the last thing we want to do is endorse an outdated (and lopsided) rule. You certainly don't want one dad to feel like he's doing more than his fair share.

If you are going to ask parents for money, ask both sets, and be sure to tell them you're asking for help from the other side. As with any wedding, don't expect them to say yes, and don't make them feel like they're obligated. Simply because of financial ability, one family might put in more cash than the other. That's okay, as long as you make sure the other family doesn't feel like they've disappointed you. Financial wedding assistance is a gift, one that should be cherished, and one that should never be expected. Your family's blessing is more valuable than anything else you might receive. This is a great time to tell your parents that.

Who proposes to whom?

Since you've bought this book, you've probably already decided you're having a wedding. However, you might still be thinking, *Is one of us supposed to pop the question?* This isn't much different from figuring out who offers to pay on a same-sex date, except that agreeing to go Dutch is much easier than agreeing to mutually propose.

As much as we'd all like to believe in the fairy tale that our soul mate takes us to the most romantic spot on the planet, pours us a glass of champagne as the sun sets, grabs our hands, and offers a ring with a promise of lifelong love if only we'll say yes . . . Well, let's put it this way: I'm still waiting for Ricky Martin to do all those things for me. Even though I haven't given up hope, the chances of it happening seem pretty slim.

Most gay couples decide together that it's time to make a lifelong commitment, usually after many discussions about finances and living together and having children. Granted, it's not the most dreamlike way of entering into wedded bliss, but it's responsible. (And just so you know, some guys and girls do make the leap and propose.) Here's a romantic suggestion: However you make the decision to get engaged, make a trip to the most beautiful spot you can think of afterward for a champagne toast.

Do you have to tell reluctant bridesmaids they have to wear dresses and shave?

If your friends aren't the frilly-dress type, you're better off forfeiting a uniform look and asking them to wear something that isn't skin-revealing. (Picture Ellen DeGeneres in a floral-print dress and heels and you might get the idea.)

Even if all you know is that you'd like the party to be dressed in blue, tell them that ahead of time. If you're adamant about women wearing dresses, and you have one friend who's dead set against it, let her know that she might look awkward standing next to the rest of the wedding party in long pants. She could go either way, but chances are, she'll be more concerned about pleasing you than she will be about following in Katharine Hepburn's footsteps. Respect whatever choice she makes. After all, you're an unconventional couple. Let your attendants be that way, too.

How do two control freaks compromise?

It happens, and, unlike that china pattern you registered for, it's not pretty. The obvious solution would be to simply hire a wedding coordinator to decide on the details, but then you'd have to relinquish the control you wanted in the first place.

This is a delicate situation because fights over wedding planning are extremely emotional. There's really only one good answer and that's to make the affair a fifty-fifty split; for example, one of you handles the reception, the other, the ceremony. No questions, no criticisms. You can, however, answer a guest's query with, "I'm not sure what kind of flowers they are. Bill was in charge." When it all comes down to "I do," chances are you'll forget about everything else. As for how to decide on who takes charge of what? Try a good analyst, a good lawyer, or a good old-fashioned coin toss.

Do you need two maids of honor/two best men?

Even if both of you have the same best friend, it's a good idea to have an attendant for each of you. Weddings, despite being about the two of you, are also very personal times. You'll want someone to confide in when you're worried you've gained too much weight, when you're certain your partner won't like what you've decided to wear, when you can't bear to have one more conversation with his parents, and when you're so mad at her you want to call the whole thing off.

If you have separate best friends, it's even more important, because you'll want that person to stand up for you. If you don't get along with your parents, all the more reason to have support from your adopted family. And at that moment right before you walk down the aisle, there's nothing more valuable than having a cherished friend hold your hand.

You've decided to have a bachelor/bachelorette party. Are two really needed?

Basically, that depends on the theme of the party. If you're breaking with tradition completely (these parties originated as celebrations to honor the groom's last days as a free man), then one is sufficient. Although, in that case, it's more of a, well, party, than anything else.

If you take a more customary approach to these affairs, however, two's a good idea. It's a way for your friends to honor you and the love and happiness they feel for you at this time in your life. A little tradition can be fun, too. Some couples like having their pals take them out to share personal stories, to reminisce about the past, and, yes, even to ogle strippers. Here, too, separate "entertainers" are a definite yes. The whole ritual is about fantasy, and that might not work when your partner tells you the dancer's hot. Like most engaged couples, you'll actually end up coming home realizing how happy you are to be giving up the single life.

Two men want a traditional affair, including a walk down the aisle.
Which groom gets the honors and who walks him down?

This dilemma comes up more often than you'd think. Unlike gay women having a wedding, where it doesn't seem strange to walk down the aisle, most people don't expect men to take that step.

Often the answer's a simple one, because only one guy wants that role. In that case, if he's on good terms with his dad, go all the way and be traditional about it. Ditto both parents for a Jewish affair. If he's not on good terms with his parents, or Dad's not comfortable in that role, a best man or any close friend makes a great option. If both guys want to walk down the aisle, take a cue from many women and go down arm in arm. After all, you decided to take this bold step together—now do it literally. Remember, in today's world of metrosexuals and gym-perfect bods, you'll probably cause gasps and more than a few tears as the guests see how beautiful you look.

Is it okay for two women to throw two bouquets?

Like the dances, this tradition is often among the first to go at gay weddings. Many women see it as silly, even insulting, especially because it's a ritual that's intended to determine who gets married next—gay weddings are still developing and there's no one pressuring young gay women to find a mate. (In all fairness, many straight women now forgo the toss.)

That aside, throwing a bouquet's just plain fun, and it harks back to what many dreamed about when they were little. Our suggestion: Yes, throw two bouquets. No one's going to think it's tacky, and you can just think of it as twice as much fun. (It should be noted that if you have a lot of gay men at the wedding, they'll dive for those flowers like children for piñata candy.)

And what do men toss?

Assuming you're not a transvestite or dressed in drag, tossing a garter does seem a little awkward—and might send your male guests running for cover.

So what *do* you throw? The safest options are black ties or boutonnieres. Of course, there's always another option that's a sure crowd-pleaser. A bouquet! Yes, guys can do it, too. If you're the masculine type, skip the baby's breath and throw in some manly blooms, like sweet williams.

What do two women do if only one wants a diamond engagement ring?

One of you would be happy with a kabbalah bracelet, while the other wants a one-carat-diamond-ring spectacular. Who pays for the sparkler? The easiest solution would be to let the giver foot the bill (or put her foot down and just say no), but since a wedding ring can be one of life's most treasured gifts, it shouldn't be denied, nor should it be the responsibility of only one of you. Split the tab, or, better yet, let Ms. Taylor pay for the ring herself. That's not being stingy, it's being fair and practical. In an age when women are demanding—if not necessarily getting—equal rights, this is as good an opportunity as any to make a statement that one person shouldn't have to bear an unequal amount of any wedding cost. Your straight friends might even take a cue from your example.

Do two guys, and in some cases, two women, wear matching attire?

While it's easy to take your cue from those male-male cake toppers you'll undoubtedly be spotting, save the clone look for the Chelsea Boys. Just as it would look funny to sport identical dresses, two people are going to look odd in the same rented tuxes. To borrow a hetero expression, you're getting married, not attached at the hip.

Wear something different from each other, but similar in style and formality. After all, if one of you opts for black tie and the other black jeans, you're more than likely to give off the impression that the affair is not of equal importance to both of you. Most male couples go with, say, suits and ties, but of their own choosing. And you can certainly go more casual or formal as best befits your wedding. Do, however, consult each other on attire. You're going to look classy as all get-out if your outfits have a coordinated look.

Who gives the first toast at a lesbian wedding?

Seems like a no-brainer, doesn't it? Whoever feels motivated first should just get up and speak. But a wedding is not a typical get-together, and you'll find that guests won't want to step on anyone else's toes. Since you don't have a best man to automatically assume it's his duty to say a few words, things get more complicated. The maid of honor? What if you have two?

Set aside a few minutes at least a week before the ceremony (speeches make people nervous and they need time to practice), pick a person you mutually agree upon, and let your choice know you'd be honored if he or she gave the first toast. Also, mention at what point the toast should begin—usually, right before the food is served. And if you have a band or DJ, make sure they know to tone down the music so that all ears are tuned in to the praises of the two of you.

Who's listed as host on the invitations? And whose name goes first?

If either set of parents is paying for the wedding, or a good chunk of it, common courtesy calls for you to list their names as hosts. (Ditto for any engagement parties.) If that's not the case for the two of you, however, simply put your own names down as the inviters.

The next challenge is how to announce who's getting hitched to whom—traditionally, the parents announce the marriage of their daughter to someone else's son. There are a million ways you could go on this one—consult your astrological charts, say, or use a feng shui guide to tell you which name is more harmonious in front of the other. But here's a perfect opportunity for you to KISS (Keep It Simple, Stupid): List your names alphabetically. Now you can go back to worrying about more important details, like making sure the crab cakes match the color of the linens.

Who carries whom over the threshold?

Whoever's stronger and has no history of back pain. Otherwise, make it a joint leap of faith.

"Our advice? Breathe, then call the few people in your life with whom you most want to share the news."

The Life of the Party: Choosing Your Attendants

There's a tendency, when you've just become engaged, to call everyone you know with the good news and ask them to take part in the ceremony. That's incredibly sweet—and incredibly stupid. Before you know it, you'll have thirty-seven bridesmaids or twenty-two ushers, your sister and your best friend will both swear you asked her to be maid of honor, and your two dads will want to know what they should wear when they walk you down the aisle. Of course, none of this will matter to you; you'll have already eloped to Belgium in order to get away from the pandemonium you've caused.

Our advice? Breathe, then call the few people in your life with whom you most want to share the news. Wait a few weeks before deciding on your attendants. You'll have come down to earth by then, and you will have had time to make some logical choices.

First, decide on how many attendants you (a) would like, and (b) can afford (every attendant is another guest). Your honor attendant, as stated earlier, can be anyone—male, female, mother, father; what's important to remember is that it be someone whose presence will mean the world to you. In addition, make sure the person you ask *wants* to be in the wedding. You might be incredibly close to your friend Eileen but have failed to realize (or have forgotten) that she's in the middle of writing her dissertation. This is one of those times when it's not just about you. Everyone in your wedding party will be spending a lot of time, energy, and money to participate. It's essential that they be as happy to take part in the day as you are in having them there.

Also, be clear when asking people to be a part of your wedding that your feelings won't be hurt if they say no. There's nothing more upsetting than hearing stories about a wedding where a relative of the bride felt compelled to say yes to being a bridesmaid, even though she had to rely on credit to pay for her dress and transportation, and took extra time off from work so she could attend pre-parties. In situations such as this, the person usually ends up feeling manipulated into taking part in the ceremony, and guilty for not being more happy about the wedding. And those feelings inevitably rub off on the ones getting married.

If you sense this might be the case with people whose participation you'd cherish, tell them you'd love for them to be a part of your wedding, but that their presence alone would be the best gift they could offer. And mean it! Don't take it personally if they decline. Keep in mind that you can always give them the option of doing a reading, staffing the guest book, or any other smaller task that will make them feel included.

A couple of other factors to consider when choosing your attendants: You don't have to ask someone to be your best man simply because you were his. If you've grown apart, if his taking on the responsibility means rescheduling the wedding, or if you've always had your heart set on your brother standing up for you, by all means go with your gut. If the guy's truly a good friend, he'll understand.

Even though you might not be particularly close to her relatives, don't balk when she asks if her sisters can be part of the wedding party. These people are very close to her; they're about to become your family, and now's as good a time as any to practice keeping the peace. Besides, she's probably not so crazy about a few members of your clan.

It's considered rude and unethical to "fire" an attendant. If there are people in the wedding party who are clearly unhappy (they don't like their outfits, they think the venue's rotten, they consider gay weddings a farce), sit them down and politely ask them if they'd rather not be a part of the ceremony, or if there's anything you can do to make their role more enjoyable. You might find that the cause of their grief is minor (they're having boyfriend troubles and can't focus), or serious (they're having boyfriend troubles and can't focus). Either way, if you sense they want out, let them off the hook. If you can't find a replacement, don't panic. Having one less attendant won't hurt the wedding. Having an unhappy one will.

Go Ahead, Make Their Day

All those guys and girls in your party have spent months listening to you ramble on about catering costs, floral frustrations, and heavenly honeymoons (the one part of the wedding they *don't* get to enjoy). Do yourself—and them—a favor and put aside an evening, or an entire weekend, just for the members of the wedding. Tell your attendants that anything related to your ceremony will be a forbidden subject during the allotted time.

Some options:

- *Day spa.* Take everyone to a spa for manicures, pedicures, massages, or facials. Gay guys aren't likely to flinch when they hear you've arranged a Day of Beauty for each of them. A great option for girls, too, is to arrange for a makeup artist or hairstylist to arrive on the day of the wedding to fix them up. It's one less thing for them to worry about, and it also helps you—you'll be relieved of stressful last-minute panic attacks over unruly hair and cosmetics calamities.

- *Wine tasting.* You probably all want a drink right about now, so if you live anywhere near a winery, make it a day trip. In addition to being a heck of a lot of fun, it's a great way to relax and bond over wine and cheese on the vineyard grounds. One exception: Don't go this route if a member of your party is a nondrinker. Telling him he gets to be the designated driver isn't likely to make him feel special. If he opts out everyone will be disappointed, and if he goes along and doesn't imbibe, he's most likely going to feel that this is one more activity geared toward pleasing you.

- *Bridesmaids/groomsmen luncheon.* Tell your party to set aside one Saturday afternoon, give them an idea about what to wear, then surprise them all by having cabs pick them up and take them to a chic restaurant in town. Just when they thought this was going to be another weekend afternoon spent going over hors d'oeuvres options, they'll be treated to a great meal instead. They deserve a break today.

- *Sexes and the city.* If you can afford it, one of the nicest ways to treat your attendants is to plan a weekend away. Popular spots for quick getaways include New York; Vegas or Atlantic City; Colorado for skiing and Miami for beaching; or, depending on the personality of your party, anywhere in California, from Beverly Hills to Big Sur. Wherever you go, rent a couple of rooms and plan to order up a lot of room service. And make sure your single friends have time to check out the local dating scene. You might be able to put your newfound wedding knowledge to use sooner than you think.

If money's tight, remember, the above ideas are merely suggestions. Wine tasting's too expensive? Buy a couple of bottles and have everyone over to your house for a night of scary movies and pillow fights. A luncheon not in your budget? Surprise them with a feast you cooked yourselves—just don't let them do the dishes afterward! The only rule when planning a party for your party is that, for a short time, they get to be the life of it.

The Guess List

Figuring out who to invite to your wedding can be one of the most stressful duties the two of you will endure. The last thing you want to do is leave someone out or hurt someone's feelings. At the same time, you don't want anyone there who's going to be the nail in the enjoyment-factor coffin. By the time you figure out who's coming, you'll probably have a better understanding as to why some people just elope.

That said, follow a few simple guidelines and you can add some fun to this planning stage.

If either set of parents has pitched in, let them have a say about who's coming. If one set of parents is paying for the whole affair, let them have a lot of say. That usually translates to a sizable chunk of guests—assuming, however, that they want the responsibility. Most parents will have a couple of "requirements," like dear Aunt Sophie and that kind young gay man at the grocery whom they think needs a couple of positive role models. If parents are dead set on inviting everyone from the country club, however, you have to say no, despite the fact that they've handed over a check.

Wedding money is a gift, not a loan, and, should the unfortunate time come, you'll have to sit them down and explain that to them. If parents are still determined to bring the bridge team, then you have to rethink the affair and tell Mom and Dad, or Dad and Dad, that you'd much rather have a small wedding with your closest friends and relatives than a large one with theirs. Of course, depending on their reaction, you may have to rethink the budget.

After you sift through the parental guest requirements, should they exist, the basic rule of thumb is that guests are divided up fifty-fifty between the two of you. Fair enough, yes. Logical, not always. Sometimes one of you needs to invite more than the other—be it due to a family contribution, more relatives, or simply because one of you has more friends.

Should you foresee a situation in which the guest lists aren't going to be even—and you're the one with the larger number—try to cut your list down to size. If it's a relative issue, carefully go through those friends you wanted to invite and see if there are some you can leave off. An evenly divided guest count makes for a much more fulfilling party.

Co-workers can be a tricky situation for any wedding, gay or straight. To a certain extent, you've got the homo-field advantage. A lot of people don't particularly want to invite their office mates to their ceremonies, but feel that it's a social responsibility. Since gay weddings have yet to be universally recognized, you're not in that position. Also, you simply may not feel comfortable having people from your office seeing you lip-locked with your partner, or you may not be out to all of them. Remember, however, that if you do invite people from your office, the rule of thumb is that you include everyone in your department, *or* just your boss, but not a select few.

KIDDIE CORNER

You are not a horrible person if you decide to have an adults-only wedding. If you go back and remember what it was like when you were a kid, you'll probably discover that you weren't always so keen about dressing up to watch two people get all mushy. Whether or not you invite children to the wedding is an entirely personal matter, and there are no rules saying when it's a requirement and when it's not. Even if you include children in your wedding party, that doesn't mean other children should automatically be invited.

What *is* required is that you let guests know if they can bring their children. If the answer's yes, write out each child's full name on the invitation. In a perfect world, if children's names didn't appear on invites, parents would know that it's an adults-only affair. But this world is far from perfect, and you're bound to get a couple of phone calls before the wedding asking if little Cindy Lee can attend (expect more than a few kid queries if word gets out your nephew's a ring bearer). Don't cave: It's never fun to be the bad guy, but should this happen, stand firm and very politely state that, as much as you'd love to include everyone in your wedding, you've made a joint decision that the ceremony's best suited for adults. If parents are traveling a long distance to be at your wedding, and they need to bring their children with them, an extremely generous and smart offer is to provide information on babysitting services in your area.

DOUBLE THEIR PLEASURE?

Many people are under the false assumption that a wedding is like a Saturday-night keg party: If they receive an invitation, it automatically means they get to bring a date. Not so. Traditionally speaking, only the people whose names are on the invitation are being asked. Once again, it's up to you as to whether or not you want (and can afford) to have people bring dates. Etiquette dictates only that married people and couples should expect their partners to be invited.

A few things to keep in mind. Before you write "and guest" on the invitation, know that, should you go this route with one person, you're going to have to do it with everyone. It's not particularly kind to decide that certain friends of yours are worthy of bringing along an escort, while others . . . well, you don't particularly like their taste in dates and would rather they show up solo.

There are other areas where "and guest" gets mucky. For example, is another gay wedded couple considered "married" and therefore deserving of having both names on the invite, or do you write "and guest" for the one you don't know as well, while at the same time treating your legally married friends equally? For reasons such as these, the label's best avoided.

Instead, every person who's invited to your wedding should have his or her name mentioned on the invitation. That means if your married friends Suzie and Tyler Straightlace are invited, both names are listed. Don't assume Suzie will automatically know her husband is being asked to attend, and vice versa. Similarly, if your friend Doug has been with his partner, Ramone, for ten years but they don't live together, call Doug and ask for Ramone's address. Then send him a separate invitation.

One of the most awkward situations when planning the guest list occurs when you desperately want to invite a close friend, but either detest the person he or she is living with or simply don't know the other person very well. Often, in this case, people choose not to invite the "insignificant other." Bad decision. When you alienate someone's partner, for whatever reason, you're basically telling your friend that you don't support his or her life-mate decisions—an especially harsh statement at a time when you want people to support your own togetherness.

Go by the book in this case: If a friend or relative is living with someone, automatically invite that person, no matter what your personal feelings. The only nontacky alternative is to invite neither, which, of course, leaves you without that special friend on your big day. If you're having second thoughts about this rule, think about what life is like as a gay person in our society, and all the times you've been left out of social activities simply because someone didn't approve of you. Do you really want to be the one who's now doing the excluding?

Just as with children, expect people to contact you asking if they can bring a date. Once again, be firm in your negative response. Be reasonable, sympathetic, understanding, and supportive. And if none of that works, tell them this book told you it was okay to say no!

THE B LIST

You've planned for a hundred guests and only fifty have RSVP'd? Don't panic; consult your B list. Unlike a pretentious nightclub, a "B" or "sub" list for a wedding is a must. Simply put, as with any party, not everyone will be able to attend your wedding. If you've got room for twenty-five more, that means those people you really wanted to invite but couldn't, because of budget or other constraints, can now be invited. (Worried they'll "catch on" that they weren't first choice? Hopefully, true friends will understand how expensive and complicated weddings are, and merely be thrilled you thought of them.)

Do make sure the ones you haven't heard from don't plan on attending. If they haven't RSVP'd by the requested date (usually a month to two weeks before the big day), call or e-mail them and ask if they're coming. Some people don't understand the importance of a quick response; others forget. There's nothing tacky about reaching out to remind someone. Once you've got the clearance for more people, send them invites if there's time. If it's too rushed, call them and tell them you're having a wedding, you know it's last-minute, but you'd be thrilled if they could join you. No further explanation is needed.

AND SPEAKING OF E-MAIL . . .

The etiquette police have yet to tackle Internet correspondence (they're still trying to figure out if it's okay to drag out cell phones on dates), so common sense is the enforcer here. When it comes to a wedding, how would you feel if the invitation arrived via e-mail? Not so hot, right? The consensus on every end of the wedding spectrum is that there's nothing quite so special as an old-fashioned mailperson-delivered note. That's a message that comes straight from the heart.

Having a Wonderful Time, Why Aren't You Here?

Even the happiest occasions can be laced with sadness, and a wedding is no exception. As much as we'd like to only report on the joyous aspects of planning, it's important that we say a few things about the possible downside of your big day. With hope, you'll encounter none of the problems below. With time, these problems will (hopefully) not exist. For now, how to deal when the news is bad.

IT'S A GAY WEDDING, NOT A REAL ONE!

The most common of the unfortunate guest situations, friends and relatives who don't take your wedding seriously can, in many ways, be the hardest people to cope with. On the one hand, they're supportive of your relationship and think it's swell that you're gay. These are often the people you've turned to when you've had a lovers' spat, and who have included your partner in parties, weekend outings, even their own weddings.

However, when you ask them to be a witness at a celebration of your love, they laugh it off as a trendy or fun way to make a statement, not a lifelong commitment. These are the people who don't RSVP but still show up, who don't bother bringing a gift or pay attention to the dress code, or who bring along an uninvited guest because, in their opinion, the more the merrier.

You can't force anyone to take your wedding seriously; even if you haul everyone off to Canada to make it legal, the act will most likely be dismissed as a stunt—an impressive stunt, but a stunt nevertheless. What you can do is stand firm when anyone's behavior is less than acceptable. If Aunt Dipso says she won't be able to attend your wedding, then calls the day before to ask what time the cocktail hour is, don't rearrange the seating chart to fit her in. Tell her the obvious: She said she wasn't coming, and, unfortunately, you can't squeeze her in at such a late date. The more you pander to this personality type, the longer it will take for your commitment to be taken seriously. If the person behaving badly is someone whose wedding you attended, or if it's someone whom you've been to weddings with, remind him or her of the protocol exhibited on previous occasions. When Corey Dimlit phones you for permission to bring along his weekend housemates, tell him no. If he seems perplexed or upset, ask him if he would have brought along guests at the last "real" wedding he attended. The silence you'll hear on the other end is the sound of Corey's brain doing the math.

Another way to reinforce your wedding's legitimacy? Have loved ones spread the word. Your reluctant relations will be more responsive to your wedding if they receive calls from other friends, relatives, and Mom and Dad telling them about rehearsal dinners and engagement parties, or e-mailing with vital information, like a map to the reception site, a wedding website, or a reminder that the affair is black tie. Like a wedding itself, going public with the news is the surest way to make it an official event.

LOST IN TRANSLATION

Another unwelcome wedding surprise may be people who boycott your wedding altogether. An especially hurtful act, it's even worse when the absentee guest is someone you never knew had trouble dealing with your homosexuality, your partner, or the idea of a same-sex ceremony. Unfortunately, the problem's more common than people think. Uncle Arthur has always appeared as if he's okay with your situation. You love the guy, and you can't wait for him to see you in that wedding dress. Then time passes by and you never get an RSVP. You leave a message on his machine and he doesn't call back. Finally, your mother hears from Aunt Ruby that, as much as your uncle loves you, he believes that God never intended for two women to share their lives together, and he's going fishing on the day of your wedding. As if that isn't hurtful enough, you then hear that, out of respect for her husband's beliefs, Aunt Ruby won't be attending, either.

Should you find yourself in this unfortunate situation, the best advice is to grin and share it. Meaning, feel free to tell your uncle how painful his decision is, remind him that he'll be missing out on one of the most important days of your life, and then let it go. You're going to find that having a gay wedding means discovering a lot about people that you didn't already know. Not all of it will be rosy. That's life, it happens at all weddings, gay or straight, and it's all part of the learning process as you embark on your new future. Whatever happens, good or bad, you'll wind up the wiser for it.

THE UNINVITED

The reverse scenario is deciding when it's okay not to invite someone to your wedding. Let's say you've got a lot of siblings, and they've known about your homosexuality for years. Mom and Dad invite your partner to every holiday get-together, and when you announce your engagement over dinner one evening, everyone rejoices over the upcoming June wedding between Allen and Tom.

Everyone, that is, except your sister Naomi. For whatever reasons (religious, social, her own insecurities), your sister has never approved of your situation, and the wedding only fuels her fire. Your partner has put his foot down and doesn't want your sister anywhere near your wedding. If you don't invite her, however, your mother will feel the wedding's incomplete, and what's more, you're hoping that if your sibling can only see the two of you saying your vows, somehow her homophobia will disappear.

As much as you'll hear that not inviting a family member to a wedding is inflicting a wound that could last a lifetime, a relative whose presence will ruin the event—she'll be disorderly, she'll make fun of the affair, or her simply being around the two of you will be a constant reminder of the prejudice you face—should not be invited. Considering the fact that she probably doesn't want to attend in the first place, you'll be doing both of yourselves a favor. Yes, you should always try to resolve the issue first, but a wedding day shouldn't have to equal an equal-rights battle.

The most important thing to remember when deciding on whether or not to invite someone is how important it is that he or she witness your ceremony. You can't change the world overnight; as you make up your guest list, come to terms with the fact that some of your invitees may not have conquered their ignorance of your commitment. Once you ask people to attend, do it with all your heart, and accept them for the lovably flawed human beings they are—in other words, the way people accept you.

THE
12-STEP
WEDDING
PLANNER

Barb & Heather

WHO: Barb, twenty-seven, and Heather, twenty-nine, Rhodes-Weaver.

WHEN: Saturday, July 1, 2000.

WHERE: The Kline Galland Mansion, Seattle, Washington. A five o'clock ceremony in the garden and indoor reception immediately following. Eighty guests were treated to a buffet dinner of salmon, crab cakes, and vegetarian dishes.

ALL DRESSED IN WHITE: The women both wore designer wedding dresses.

BACKED BY BLACK: The six bridesmaids wore dark dresses they picked out themselves. "We wanted them to be able to wear their outfits again," says Barb.

WE'LL DRINK TO THAT: They opened up the bar early so everyone in the wedding party would lighten up for the formal photographs.

CUSTOM COMFORTS: A rehearsal dinner, bachelorette party, four ushers, two ring bearers, a flower girl, a first dance, a father–daughter dance, two bouquet tosses, and a DJ who played the Macarena.

CUSTOM QUOTE: "If I knew the wedding was going to be so traditional, I wouldn't have come," joked one guest.

YOU'VE GOT VEIL: The officiant was a friend who got ordained over the Internet.

GIFT-FRIENDLY: The couple registered at Bed Bath & Beyond because it was the only store they could find that would list them as a wedding couple.

WHAT THEY OVERCAME: Determined to have a female–female cake topper, Barb's mother and sister bought two cake toppers at Wal-Mart, pried off the male figurines at the store, and glued the brides together.

THANKS FOR THE MEMORIES: On Monday the couple took thirty remaining guests rafting; they had a cookout on the Fourth of July.

THEY DID: On August 1, 2003, Barb and Heather made it official by getting married in Victoria, British Columbia.

*N*ow that we've gone through a lot of your ceremony pre-liminaries, we thought it would be helpful to give you a step-by-step guide on the nuts and bolts of your wedding. The following twelve categories cover the basic details you need to address and resolve to make your ceremony complete. Assuming you've got a year to plan your big day (the average length of an engagement), you'll want to decide these factors starting around four months into planning, and be able to check them all off by the six-month mark. Of course, not everyone has exactly a year to plan, so adjust these sections to fit into your own schedule. To guide you further, we've listed these details in order of importance. Spent too much time deciding on the music and flowers? Relax, transportation and grooming concerns can spill over into the last few months before you say "I do." However, it's best to get as many of these tasks accomplished on schedule as you can, so the days leading up to the wedding will be as stress-free as possible. Get set, get on your calendar marks, and get going. Your wedding will go off without a hitch if you stick to the program and take it one day at a time.

Step 1.
Reception Food and Drink

What's the first thing that comes to mind when you think of the last great dinner party you went to? Chances are, you remember the meal. Face it: Despite what all those diet books tell you, food *is* love, and it should be prepared that way at your reception. In the months to come, your guests might not remember your centerpieces, they might not remember the name of the swing band, they may not even remember those incredibly touching vows you spent three weeks working on with a professional acting coach. They will, however, remember the food. That's why, as soon as you've booked your site, the first thing you want to decide on is what you'll be serving. In order to eat, drink, and be "Mary," you've got to come up with a meal plan.

Feeding Frenzy: What a Caterer Does

The caterer is, of course, the nucleus of your reception-party meal. Depending on your site, the duties can vary greatly. A caterer can be one person or it can be an entire company consisting of cooks, wait staff, and bartenders. If, for example, you're having your wedding in a banquet hall, the caterer (in this case probably a company) might be responsible for all food and drink, plus the wedding cake. They may also provide tables and chairs, as well as all prep work and cleanup services. Should the site and caterer go hand in hand, you'll want to make sure you're as happy with the food as you are with the hall you've rented.

If your reception's being held at your home, you'll be responsible for finding a caterer on your own. In this case, you may have to hire bartenders separately, you'll probably be responsible for providing your own tables and chairs (most caterers can give you tips on where to rent), and you might need to find a separate baker for the cake.

Choose a restaurant reception, and chances are pretty good the "caterer" will be the staff. Make sure you love the restaurant's food—if you've eaten there a thousand times, it's a safe bet you're not going to be disappointed. If you pick a restaurant based on someone's recommendation or on the decor alone, however, arrange ahead of time to sample the menu, either by eating there a few times (don't order the same thing), or arranging a food sampling with the chef. Relying on friends' assurances alone should be avoided, no matter how many *Bon Appétits* they have stacked on their coffee table. You want the meal to reflect your personal style. What's nouvelle cuisine to one person is hors d'oeuvres on a plate to another. Like your outfits, your music, and your guests, the type of food you serve, and how you serve it, represents all the things you love in life.

AT YOUR SERVICE: HOW TO FIND THE PERFECT CATERER

Ask around. Call up recently wedded friends and relatives and find out who catered their weddings and whether or not they were happy with the service. Ditto any acquaintances who've thrown a catered party recently, or who might have gone to a catered get-together. Think back to any event you attended where the food was great. Maybe your office uses a dynamite catering service. If there is a restaurant whose food's unbeatable, call the place and see if it caters. Even if it doesn't, the chef might put you in touch with his or her favorite foodie. Be sure to ask any vendors whom you're already working with if they have recommendations—chances are pretty good that your site manager's dealt with a lot of catering companies. Finally, check your local yellow pages or do a Google search for caterers in your city. A few sites we like are brides.com, modernbride.com, and weddingchannel.com, all of which should be able to direct you to professionals in your area. If you'd rather not deal with telling people you're a same-sex couple, rainbowweddingnetwork.com offers a state-by-state list that includes only gay-friendly companies.

Once you've gotten a few leads, ask them for referrals. If The Pretentious Palate can't dig up at least two or three references, you're better off going with an all-Blimpie menu. At least you'll know what you're getting for your money. Now's the time to go over all types of options with companies, to see if they can accommodate your budget and still pull off the kind of party you want. Listen to their suggestions, but be firm on your demands. If you're a deviled eggs fan and the caterer insists that crayfish is the appetizer du jour, go to the next company on your list.

Ask the caterer about service; for example, how will the wait staff dress? Inquire about how flexible the company is with the types of people who'll do the serving. Will they send all men if you prefer? Women? (This is where having a referral is an especially great source. Ask former clients what the staff were like. Were they friendly or stuffy? Quiet or flirtatious? Even though the servers are not your guests, they're still going to be members of the wedding. You want to make sure your personalities don't clash.) Does the caterer charge by the night, per number of guests, or for a certain number of hours? If the latter, what do overtime fees cost? Will they clean up, and what supplies, if any, will you have to provide yourselves or rent? If you're having your wedding at someone's home, tell them if you have a dishwasher and any cookware that could be of use. You might be able to save money if you supply your own espresso machine.

If you like what you're hearing, ask the caterer to fax or e-mail you a couple of sample menus. If they refuse, or show any reluctance ("We won't know what to serve until we make peace with the space"), hang up and dial the next number on your list. Before you make plans to meet with the caterer or have any more consultations, tell them you're having a gay wedding and make sure they're comfortable with it. At the risk of outing fine party planners everywhere, many people in the food business have, um, "personal experience" with homosexuality, so the number of caterers who are either homophobic or uneasy serving gay guests should be minimal. This is especially true in large urban areas. Still, should you sense any reluctance on their part, or if they tell you that certain members of their staff might feel awkward working at your wedding, move on. A bigoted server at your local restaurant is bad enough; a bigoted server at your reception is a recipe for disaster.

SERVICE STATION: OPTIONAL DINING CHOICES

If you still haven't decided what kind of meal you'll be serving, figure it out now. Much of this will depend on the time of day your ceremony is held (you're probably not going to have a three-course meal after a 9 A.M. wedding). There are, however, different options to consider for all times of the day. Here, a basic rundown:

10 A.M.: breakfast

Most popular for at-home affairs, wedding breakfasts can be as elegant as anything—crêpes and croissants—or as casual as the two of you—waffle station, anyone? For drinks, Bloody Marys, mimosas, or Bellinis are popular options to go along with juice, coffee, and tea. Whatever you choose, you're bound to save a lot of money on liquor. A more common morning reception is a wedding brunch, served a bit later (from noon till about four), and with a few more food options, like omelets and cheese platters. Wedding cake is perfectly appropriate for breakfast or brunch, though guests probably won't feel cheated if you opt not to have one.

Noon–2 P.M.: lunch

A wedding lunch can be held anywhere, from your best friend's pad to a swanky restaurant. You can go either buffet-style or sit-down, supply your guests with premium liquors or opt for wine and a champagne toast. Here again, the menu can be cold-cuts-casual or caviar-chic. A word of caution: If there's no set time limit on lunch, guests might drink more than you think. Remember, they're starting early. Close the bar at a designated hour or your party might turn into punch-drunk love.

5–7 P.M.: cocktail party

Five o'clock might seem early to start a cocktail party, but it's a good way to let guests know not to expect a full meal. Hors d'oeuvres are the food of choice here, though keep in mind that, contrary to popular belief, this may not be the most inexpensive route. Constant chatter means the glasses keep getting refilled, and, ideally, there should never be a lull between passed canapés. Guests often treat cocktail parties as smorgasbords of bite-sized bits and mixers to mingle over. That said, you can always skip the sushi for something more economical, like prosciutto and melon and, yes, the ever-popular pigs-in-a-blanket. Another cost cutter: Serve stationary hors d'oeuvres instead of passed platters.

6–9 P.M.: dinner

It's the most popular dining option for weddings and, not surprisingly, the most expensive. Regardless of what you're serving or where, guests arriving for a dinner reception will expect to leave with a full stomach. Wedding dinners are often accompanied by a cocktail hour beforehand—a great way for people to meet if you're having a sit-down meal. The food is entirely up to you (beef, chicken, fish) and your budget, though make sure you provide a vegetarian dish for the non-meat-eating guests.

OFF THE CLOCK

None of the above dining choices is written in stone. People throw afternoon wedding teas (a great idea if you don't plan on serving alcohol), which are an inexpensive and charming way of celebrating togetherness. Others throw all-night-diner bashes (your Atkins-loving friends can order the blue-cheese-and-eggs special), and still others throw dessert parties. It's all about personality, and as long as you provide snacks and sips, you're in the clear to go your own way.

THE FIVE BASIC FOOD GROUPS

So you don't feel like an idiot when the caterer starts throwing dining terms at you, here's a list of the five most common types of service:

Buffet-style
The food is placed on one side of the room, and guests line up to choose what they want. Buffet dinners are great because there's more leeway as to when you eat, you don't get stuck with something you're allergic to, and you can have as much or as little food as you want. On the flip side, you lose a bit of formality when guests serve themselves, lines can take forever (remember how everyone rushed the Cap'n Crunch station back at the dorms?), and you don't have as much control over the pacing of the wedding. Another important consideration: Buffet dinners are not necessarily cheaper than sit-down meals; attractive preparation usually means extra food displayed, and big eaters will go back for seconds and thirds. If you're only going for the buffet because you're assuming it's a bargain, talk to the caterer first. They may offer a cheaper seating option.

Family-style

At this toned-down version of the buffet, servers bring platters of food to each table, which guests pass among themselves (kind of like Chinese takeout back home).

American-style

Servers prepare the plates of food in the kitchen, then place them on your table. If you're getting a sense of déjà vu reading that definition, it's because American is the service style common in most restaurants. When the waitress at your favorite coffee shop brings you a side of hash browns, that's American.

French-style

The servers prepare the food on a stand next to the guest tables before serving individual plates (you'll see variations on this at local Mexican restaurants; we're not sure what caused the alliance).

Russian-style

At this most formal type of table service, white-gloved servers bring courses around one at a time, and serve to guests individually. There is such an air of distinction to this kind of service that we guarantee the table will still to a hush each time the gloved one returns.

GEE, YOUR HAIR SMELLS TERRIFIC: KEEPING FOOD IN ITS PLACE

When planning your menu, keep the formality of your affair in mind. If you're dressed in jeans and cutoffs, then burgers and fries aren't a bad way to go. All tuxed out? Nix the Buffalo wings or you might end up paying extra to remove barbecue stains. Greasy food in general is a bad idea, so skip fried chicken or pizza—wiping your hands on the linens is not a photograph you want to be looking at years from now. As for crab, unless it's in the form of cakes, it's best left for another occasion, or until bibs become a fashion statement. And yes, your guests should also be spared of spareribs, as well as any hors d'oeuvre that takes more than one hand to navigate—peeling shrimp can be a major hassle when you're trying to look cool and collected, as can anything skewered. And where does one place those tiny sticks when the server walks away?

QUESTIONS TO ASK YOUR CATERER

1. What's the cost per person?

2. Will your main contact also be at your reception? If not, can you meet with your actual wedding-day caterer ahead of time?

3. Is it possible to "drop in" on another event the caterer's handling, to get a feel for their style?

4. What's the latest date before the wedding that you can make any changes, in either the menu choices or the number of people being served?

5. What kind of rentals does the caterer provide, if any? Also, do they set up tables, including place cards and centerpieces?

6. Will the staff break down and clean up, or will you be responsible?

7. If the caterer doesn't supply rental equipment, do they have a reliable contact for you to call?

8. Does the caterer provide the cake, or do you need to handle that separately? Will the caterer allow you to bring in a cake from another baker, without being charged a cake-cutting fee?

9. Does the caterer provide liquor, or can you get it yourselves? If they do provide it, how many drinks will a bottle of hard alcohol serve? Wine? Champagne?

10. Will the caterer have enough time to plan your wedding according to your wishes? (If they're handling Dolly Parton's clambake on the same day, you'll probably want to go with your second choice.)

11. Are gratuities included in your bill, or will you have to pay for them separately?

12. How much do you need to pay up front (never agree to pay the full amount), and what's the policy if you have to postpone or cancel the wedding?

13. Are there any "hidden" charges that haven't been discussed? (Make sure everything's covered in your contract or letter of agreement, and that no extra costs can be tacked on without your permission. If a juicer's purchased at the last minute, you don't want to get stuck with the bill.)

14. Will they feed the band, DJ, photographer, videographer? And are they charged for the same amount as guests? (While it's considered good form to feed on-site vendors, they don't have to have the same three-course meal your guests are being served.)

15. Is the cute bartender dating anyone? (It's always nice to be thinking of your single friends at the wedding.)

Liquor License

TIPS ON SIPS

Here, some tried-and-true money savers as you decide on liquor:

- *Red, white, and you.* Statistics show that people drink less red wine than white, so if you want to save, stick to Cabernet instead of Chardonnay. Just keep the guests away from your white dress.
- *Bait and switch.* Having an open bar? Tell the bartenders to start with a top-shelf liquor, then, unless it's requested, switch to Smirnoff when Cousin Lushious orders her third martini. If she notices, the drink's probably already on the small side—you save either way!
- *And speaking of switch.* Martini glasses tend to come in three sizes: small (the kind that Nick and Nora used to drink out of), medium (most restaurants use this size), and supersized (for the McDrinkers among you). Stick to medium. When guests drink, they tend to judge their intake by how many glasses they have, not how many ounces they consume.
- *Name your poison.* Having a signature drink ("Bill and Ted's Excellent Elixir") might seem like an extravagant waste, but if it's a frozen concoction, all that ice and juice will fill guests up more quickly than you think. Translation: They'll drink less, dudes.
- *Wine before beer, and you'll feel queer . . .* There are all sorts of theories about what types of drinking patterns cause the fewest headaches, but one thing's a given: Serve guests soft alcohol (wine, beer, champagne) and they're less likely to order hard alcohol later. Will you save on the premium brands if you offer guests wine right away? Absolut!
- *The wine whine.* On a similar note, fine wines can be quite expensive. Don't assume that just because you've eliminated the hard stuff, you're going to save money. Keep the grape stuff in the midrange (eight to twelve dollars), or you might end up spending more than you would have for a full bar.
- *The glass is half full.* Despite what you learned on *Dynasty*, even some of the most sophisticated people on the planet aren't champagne fans. Don't overdo it. Many people only drink it at weddings because it's traditional. A

word to the wise? Fill up glasses halfway instead of three-quarters. If Joan Collins shows up (or her alter ego drag queen), she can always order another.

- *Downsizing.* Not all wineglasses are created equal. Opt for the smaller version—if you're having the reception catered, ask if they have them. If they don't, find out where you can purchase them on the cheap. You're not being stingy, you're thinking big when it comes to a small budget. Whereas you can typically get about five drinks from a bottle of wine, use smaller glasses and that total turns into an easy seven up.

- *A case of consumption.* At an open bar, you're generally charged either a flat rate for the night, or by consumption (you're billed for each drink poured). Unless your guests are big-time drinkers and/or the wedding's on the weekend, when they can afford to drink more, choose the latter. Also, sometimes caterers tack on an extra fee if you have a smaller number of guests. You will also probably be charged an hourly rate for the bartenders. Regardless of what you choose, check to see if the final rate includes tips and sales tax.

THE HARD SELL OF WHOLESALE

Fact: It's cheaper if you can purchase your own liquor for your party. Most caterers can even refer you to a wholesaler in your area. If that's not an option, liquor stores, in general, offer discounts for large quantities of booze. Another fact: While we strongly recommend this practice, keep in mind that you'll still want to go over the guest list carefully to make sure you buy enough. A caterer or a restaurant manager will be better equipped to deal with an unexpected shortage, but you might have no other option than to break out the Mountain Dew should the booze run out. In general, think fifty bottles of wine for a hundred guests, and about twenty bottles of champagne. Hard liquor's much more difficult to assess. Go by your guests' drinking habits. Since a bottle is good for about twenty drinks, don't stock up on the Scotch if your friends are primarily of the rum-and-Coke breed. The good news here is that, even if you do go overboard, as long as you don't open the extra bottles (have an attendant or close friend make sure nothing's being wasted), you can usually return the unused bottles for a refund. Fiction: There's nothing you'd rather do the day after your wedding than shore up all the unopened bottles and haul them back to the liquor store. Either ask ahead of time if someone else can do it, or, better yet, save the stuff for an anniversary party.

DOES CORKAGE CAUSE SHRINKAGE?

Corkage fees are what restaurants charge for each bottle of wine they open. Check with the manager to see what the charge is, and if you'll still save money buying your own wine. It's all a matter of simple math: Restaurants charge more for wine than a liquor store does—in the same way that they charge more for food than your grocer—so compare a price of wine you buy yourselves with the add-on corkage fee. If the savings are considerable, purchase the wine and let the wait staff pop the corks. If the price doesn't vary much, save yourself yet another task, and let the restaurant do the shopping and the popping.

IT'S MY PARTY, AND I'LL GO DRY IF I WANT TO

Just as there's no rule that a wedding consist of a bride and groom, there's also no rule that alcohol must be served at your ceremony. The notion that liquor is needed in order to celebrate any occasion is a myth; it's been proven to be a depressant and can actually hamper people's moods. Many couples we've spoken with have opted out on serving booze, because of budget concerns, religious beliefs, problems with alcohol (their own addictions or those of close friends or relatives), or simply because they'd rather wake up the next day with glorious memories of the wedding, not the feeling that someone's drilling a hole in their head. Another thing to consider is your guests' drinking habits. Should someone drink and drive home, you could be responsible for any accidents. (Ask your site manager and/or caterer if they're insured against drunk-driving-related lawsuits.) If you do have guests who tend to imbibe too much, appoint a trusted—and sober—friend to watch over them, and make sure they've got a ride home, via taxi or someone else's car. While we'd never tell you not to serve alcohol at your ceremony, what we can say is that if you decide against it, you're not being a bad host, and you haven't breached any sort of etiquette must. To avoid any confusion, let guests know ahead of time that the wedding's dry. Cousin Ginny can always stash a flask in her purse.

THE RECEPTION AND FOOD CHECKLIST

Mark price estimates in the spaces below when you've got set choices for each category. If you're using a caterer (or consultant), refer to their estimates for any or all services they're providing. Once you're finished, write in a total in the space provided, then move on. Hang on, only eleven steps to go.

MEAL
- ❑ Breakfast/brunch
- ❑ Lunch
- ❑ Dinner
- ❑ Cocktail party
- ❑ Other _____

Estimated Cost $_____

SERVICE
- ❑ Sit-down
- ❑ Buffet
- ❑ Passed hors d'oeuvres
- ❑ Combination

Estimated Cost $_____

LIQUOR
- ❑ Soft bar (wine, beer, champagne)
- ❑ Champagne toast only
- ❑ Open bar
- ❑ Open bar, top shelf
- ❑ Other (nonalcoholic beverages, etc.) _____

Estimated Cost $_____

TOTAL COST FOR FOOD AND DRINK $_____

Congratulations! You've figured out food and drink. Now, let's conquer the cake. . . .

Step 2.
Cake

Having Your Cake and Wanting It, Too

Next to a white wedding dress, a cake is probably the most prominent symbol of a modern marriage ceremony. And why not? Wedding cakes are fabulous to look at, they're made of deliciously sweet ingredients, and they bring to mind birthdays and anniversaries and Mom's sweet-tooth love. There's something almost uniquely American about serving cake at a party; it's as if, with each bite, you're taking part in a tradition as important to our culture as church on Sunday or Thanksgiving with the relatives.

But times have changed. Not everyone attends a house of worship, some people dine out on holidays, and (holy sugar shock!) gay weddings don't always include cake. Legend has it that the wedding-cake tradition started during the Roman Empire, when a loaf of bread was broken over the bride's head. The crumbs that fell on the floor symbolized her fertility. Fact or fiction, beautiful story or clear-cut case of accepted aggression toward women, that's for you to decide. However, like many other traditional wedding customs, the cake is being rethought by gay couples saying "I do." Men aren't particularly concerned about whether or not they can produce babies, and women don't take to the idea of someone—or something—else determining their motherhood status. Who'd have thunk a cake could be a political issue?

On the flip side, as with so many other wedding traditions, the roots have long been forgotten, and gay couples are as flowered up about serving cake as most heterosexual couples. Here are a few ideas to help you rise to the occasion.

SWEET DREAMS

Should your caterer be in charge of providing the cake, you're going to have fewer options as to flavors and style. If the actual kind of cake you want isn't nearly as important as simply providing one that looks and tastes great, you're in luck: A package that includes the cake will probably save you some, um, dough. However, if you're set on a seven-tiered, fourteen-flavored cake with a marzipan rainbow flag running along the sides and chocolate-covered Stoli-soaked nuts in the middle, you might want to find your own baker. Once again, ask friends and relatives for recommendations, and think of any bakers you've used in the past. Also, go through wedding books and magazines that feature sections on cakes; if one leaps out at you, because of either the design or the flavor description, write down the name of the company that created it. If they don't offer service in your area, ask other bakers if they can create something similar in taste and design. Like any quality vendor, a good baker gets booked up far in advance. Order soon, or you might end up trying to convince your friends the Snootsons that Twinkies-tiered cakes are all the rage in Key West this season.

When you select a cake, ask about delivery options. Anything but a small, one-layer cake is probably best brought to your site by the baker, who then sets it up. If the cake is fairly simple in design, you might be allowed to collect it yourself, provided you bring someone along with you to help. Be sure the cost of delivery and setup (and possibly breakdown) is included in your final bill. Depending on when the cake arrives at your site, you might need to refrigerate it. Check with the baker, then make sure you've got adequate storage. Double-check that your cake can fit through any small entranceways (your car door, the site's hallways, the kitchen doors). We know of one couple who experienced their own Lucy-and-Ethel moment when the amazing, multilayered cake they designed themselves couldn't fit into their elevator. They had to break it apart and reassemble it at the wedding site.

TASTERS' CHOICE

These days, the flavors you can decide on for your cake are as diverse as the types of couples having weddings. There's no need to go with a traditional white or chocolate cake. People are choosing a variety of flavors and layers, from chocolate mousse to Bavarian cream to raspberry jam. They're also picking different styles, from carrot cake to cheesecake to ice cream cake. Cupcake towers have gotten popular as well. You don't need a degree in Sweets to figure out what type of cake you want. Simply decide what flavors you love, and then ask if the baker can include them. Once again, keep your guests in mind: As much as you may love peanut butter and jelly, an entire cake filled with both could stick in your friends' memories as well as their mouths. You can always reserve one layer for your favorite flavor. As for the rumor floating around that bakers have become less inclined to allow cake tastings, we hope it's untrue. You should always be allowed to sample flavors before you buy. If you leave the tasting feeling nauseous, perhaps you bit off a little more than you should have chewed.

TREAT YOURSELF

Another trend these days is to customize your cake's design. That three-tiered white-columned wedding cake you grew up with is no longer de rigueur. Similarly, before you scramble to find same-sex cake toppers (bakers can usually provide them, because figurines are frequently sold separately), know that many people are opting out on plastic guys and dolls in favor of something simpler and more elegant. Many cakes now have the names of the couple on top (not unlike a birthday cake), or forgo any inscription altogether to let the overall design take precedent. Go with whatever's meaningful. You took your first road trip in her convertible? See if your baker can find a model car to place on top of the cake. Baseball's your game? Plastic or even edible gloves can signify your perfect pitcher-and-catcher relationship. Of course, if all your life you've dreamed of being Barbie and Barbie or Ken and Ken, by all means place them on top of your sweet new world.

BAKER'S DOZEN: WEDDING-CAKE TIPS

- *Climate control.* Keep weather in mind when you decide on your cake. If your reception's outdoors, or anywhere warm, avoid buttercream frosting (it melts). Opt for something more humidity-friendly, like fondant. Tell your baker about any climate concerns beforehand.
- *Just like mom used to bake.* A homemade cake's a delicious idea, especially

TIMETABLE TIP:
If food and drink is
part of your recep-
tion-site package,
you'll automati-
cally take care of
this step in the ini-
tial stages of wed-
ding planning. If
not, nail this down
by month eight, if
possible.

if you or someone close to you is a great cook. However, a cake for twenty is one thing; a cake for two hundred, quite another. If you're having a large wedding, it's best to leave the cake making in the hands of the pros.

- *Just desserts.* We can't stress this enough. Since many guests won't eat cake (especially if you're serving a large meal and/or dessert), the three-tiers-for-a-hundred-guests average can be cut to size. You should be able to get away with each tier covering about fifty guests, especially if you ask the baker to cut the slices a bit smaller.

- *Sheet happens.* It's the oldest trick in the wedding-party book. Have a beautifully decorated small cake displayed, then a sheet cake of the same flavor stored in the back.

- *Manly, yes, but ladies like it, too.* Groom's cakes (traditionally chocolate with fruit filling or fruit on top)—once separate confections wrapped up for guests to take home—are now a common cake choice at male weddings; even women are opting for this more masculine alternative. Couples usually opt to have one each, and often in the shape of a favorite pastime or hobby. We suggest you rethink your favorite *shared* hobby.

- *The anniversary party.* Another popular wedding tradition is to freeze the top layer of your cake and eat it on your one-year anniversary. Unless you're a fan of freezer burn, serve it up for a birthday or another occasion closer to your wedding date.

- *Avoid the layered look.* Each flavor you choose will probably ratchet up the cake's price. Make sure you ask your baker about price costs before deciding on a Baskin-Robbins thirty-one-flavored theme.

- *Photo finish.* If there are no display cakes for you to look at, ask your baker to show you photographs of other wedding cakes she's designed. Also inquire if there's any design she *can't* accommodate—not everyone can make a cake in the shape of Angelina Jolie's lips.

- *Tastefully correct.* Appealing as many cake flavors are, know that some guests will have to opt out on certain ingredients. For example, many people are allergic to nuts and berries; a rum cake layer might sound like a barrel of laughs, but alert your guests. Potables are potent, glasses or not.

- *Get fresh.* Find out from your baker (and confirm on paper) when the cake will actually be made. The more popular the caterer or company, the more likely the cake's going to be laid up in their fridge. The cake should never be more than a day old.

- *Toxic shock.* Fresh flowers are a wonderful way to enhance your cake. Double-check with your baker, however, to make sure they haven't been sprayed with pesticides. You don't want a guest accidentally biting into a poisonous petunia.
- *Cutting costs.* Cakes don't always come cheap: A slice can cost from two dollars to about twelve. Unless you know you've got a crowd of sweet-eaters, think twice before splurging on the most expensive cake money can buy.

Since a baker's dozen is actually thirteen, we thought we'd throw in an extra precautionary tip for you, too. *Have a backup cake!* With the ever-so-slim possibility that something could happen to prevent your cake from getting to the church on time, find out how you can secure a last-minute sweetener. Check ahead of time for pastry shops and even grocery stores (some have cake sections) open on your wedding day. Better a last-minute sweet than a sourpuss crowd.

THE CAKE CHECKLIST

❑ Formal, tiered cake

❑ Other (ice cream cake, cupcakes, etc.) _____

Estimated Cost $_____

ANY ADDITIONAL COSTS (tips, rental fees, etc.) $_____

TOTAL COST FOR CAKE $_____

Congratulations, you've conquered the cake. Now we'll find a florist. . . .

Step 3.
Flowers

With all due respect to Marilyn Monroe and dog lovers everywhere, when it comes to weddings, flowers are a guy's and girl's best friend. Why do we love them? Let's count the ways: They look beautiful, they represent love and friendship, and they're not so hard on the olfactory senses, either. More than anything, however, flowers are the essence of romance. We give them on that first, hopeful date, we have them sent to long-distance loved ones, and we offer them as a truce to patch up a silly quarrel or spat. When it comes to matters of the heart, flowers seem to say it all.

Your wedding, then, is no exception. Love among the blooms is as much a part of ceremonies as the food and drink and what you wear. Couples agonize over daisies or daffodils, carnations or calla lilies. Centerpieces can overflow with flowers, altars are often lined with them, and reception sites can be filled with numerous kinds of floral arrangements. Chances are, no matter what style of wedding you have or where you have it, you're going to want to make your own flower statement.

For how to do it, read on. This bud's for you.

Finding Your Florist

As with any vendor, the first place to go for referrals is to people who've already been there. Ask everyone you know who their favorite florist is—now that *Sex and the City*'s off the air and *The West Wing*'s, well, over, it will give you something new to talk about around the fax machine at work. Wherever you go, stop to smell the roses . . . literally. That restaurant around the corner always has beautiful bouquets? Go in and ask who does the arrangements. You've got a friend with an immaculate garden? Chances are God wasn't his only little helper. His gardener might know the best florist in town. Even some high-class gyms have stems to sigh for. Pump the owners for information. And think back to the last time someone sent you a beautiful bouquet. Finally, whip out the yellow pages and bookmark those Googled flower sites on the Web, then ask all other vendors if they have recommendations.

As for specific websites, try citysearch.com. All you have to do is choose a city near you and type in "Florists." You'll get listings, as well as ratings, for local florists, along with information on whether or not the florist specializes in weddings. In addition, all mainstream wedding sites have directories, including brides.com, modernbride.com, and theknot.com. WeddingChannel.com's site includes photo galleries of florists' work. Scared straight? Rainbowwedding network.com lists gay-friendly florists only, though expect to find a more limited city selection.

Once you've done the prep work, it's all about the style you want and the price you can afford. Just because a florist's résumé includes Susan Lucci's Emmy Award Christening or Woody Harrelson's Hemp-Fest doesn't mean she's the right person for your ceremony. And if she immediately quotes prices way out of your range, it's time to dig a little deeper for that perfect match. You need to connect with your florist and have a similar idea of how you envision your wedding. Whereas some couples are all about flowers, others will want just a touch of scented bliss. Wherever you land on the floral scale, you're sure to find this task an experience of personal growth.

Bud of Course: Where Flowers Go

Below, a few general ideas about where you'll want to place your blooms:

- *Bouquet.* If a bouquet (or two) is in order, this is the number one floral target, and the last place you'll want to skimp.
- *Bouquets for bridesmaids.* Also a good place to prioritize. Even though a bridal bouquet is usually more elaborate than the attendants', you'll want your bridesmaids' to look ravishing. If you're including a flower girl, she'll need a basket of her own blooms.
- *Boutonnieres.* For the grooms, groomsmen, ushers, male relatives, and ring

bearers. The only "rule" regarding boutonnieres is that the grooms' look slightly different from the rest of the men's flowers—usually by adding a distinctive extra bloom.

- *Corsages.* While it's customary to give corsages to mothers of the brides (wrist or pin), we think it's a nice gesture to give flowers to all female members of the wedding party. And hey, there's no law against men carrying flowers, either. Of course, skip it for the women (and there may be many) for whom a corsage is clearly a needless accessory—long live the butch babe!

- *House of worship.* Buds brighten up any ceremony spot, and they'll look wonderful in photos. Make sure you place them in the often overlooked back of the church, for any shots taken as the wedding party enters.

- *Centerpieces.* While flowers are certainly not a requirement for centerpieces, they're an extremely popular option, and one you'll no doubt want to discuss with your florist.

- *Pews and aisle runners.* Also optional, pew and aisle runner flowers are a lovely touch. If your site is already heavily ornamented, or your budget's being stretched, it could be a touch too much.

- *Reception site.* Think about the gift table (if you have one), the cake table (ditto), and various spots around the space. How much you invest on flowers in this category is completely up to you, as well as where your reception's being held. If you're saying your vows in a garden, for example, Mother Nature's already done most of the floral planning for you.

TIPTOEING THROUGH THE TULIPS: FLORAL ADVICE

- *Sample stems.* Think your florist's da bomb? Tell him what kind of flowers you have in mind, and have him make up a sample bouquet or arrangement. It's a great way to see if you're on the same page.

- *Weatherproof.* All flowers are not created equal: Whereas sweet peas flourish in summer, hydrangeas are best suited for winter. Check with your florist to make sure your blooms are compatible with the season of your wedding.

QUESTIONS TO ASK YOUR FLORIST

1. What flowers will be in season around your wedding date? (You'll save big bucks if you don't have to import your blooms from below the border.) It helps if you have a list of flowers you love, and then can mark off the ones that will be too pricey to use.

2. Who does the actual arranging of the flowers for the wedding? If it's not your initial contact, make sure you get to meet with the person who'll be in charge. Also ask about a backup, should the florist fall ill or have any emergency that would prevent her from working on your wedding day.

3. Will the flowers be set up at the site or just dropped off? If the latter, you'll need to figure out who's going to take care of this responsibility while you tend to more important details.

4. What blooms can be substituted should the flowers you choose not be available on the day of your wedding? Make sure your alternative choice is written in the contract.

5. Do any flowers you want stain? The pollen of some blooms can smear on clothing.

6. How open is the florist to your suggestions? If you're a control freak about your wedding, you don't want to work with a "Miss My Way or the Highway." Similarly, if all you care about is that you get white roses and stay within your budget, a take-charge florist is your best bet.

7. Does your florist have any other wedding obligations on your day? If so, how many? (Just knowing that the florist has to dash off at a certain hour for another event might make some couples nervous.)

8. Is the florist familiar with your ceremony and reception sites? If a florist knows the space of your house of worship, he'll have a much better grasp of what works there and how much you should expect to pay. If the florist doesn't know your site (for example, if you're having an at-home wedding), make sure he's willing to check the space out ahead of time.

9. What flowers work best with your color scheme? Tell your florist about the look of the room, your attire, and any other style elements you've established. (This is especially helpful if you're clueless about blooms.)

10. "Do you mind if I look around the shop?" If you don't like the florist's own designs, what are the odds that you'll like what she comes up with for your wedding?

- *A room with a view.* Floral centerpieces should enhance conversation, not prevent it. Keep the blooms low so that no one's across-the-table vision is impaired.
- *The green party.* Plants are cheaper than fresh-cut flowers. Consider having them placed around your reception site to keep costs down.

TIMETABLE TIP:
If flowers are extremely important to you, start searching for a florist as soon as you've set the date. Otherwise, you can wait up till about six months before the wedding to check this off.

- *Paper roses.* Preserving your bouquet's a sentimentalist's dream—but ask the florist ahead of time if he can arrange it, or recommend someone else for the job. If you want to have your flowers and toss them, too, your florist can make a "stunt" bouquet to throw to the crowd.

- *Here's looking at-choo!* You probably know if you have any flower allergies, but what about the rest of the wedding party? Ask people what they're allergic to, in case you have to nix part of the mix. While you're at it, you might want to stay away from highly pungent blooms—it's a wedding, not a perfume counter.

- *Humane nature.* Arrange to have your flowers donated to a hospital or nursing home after the reception (and give a charitable thanks to the person who agrees to drop them off). Your flowers will end up brightening up someone else's day, too.

Deflowered Centerpieces

Want something else to sparkle on tables? Here are a few alternatives to floral bouquets that are popping up everywhere:

- *Seashells.* Especially fun if your wedding's a day at the beach.
- *Candles.* Dripping with good taste, candlelight heats up the romance factor at any reception.
- *Plant it here.* Vases of tropical leaves are gorgeous and affordable. And grass is always greener laid out on flats.
- *Fruit.* Tables of fruit can be just as festive as those baskets you receive around the holidays.
- *Just desserts.* Bakers (either your caterer or a local shop) are crafting elegant cakes and pies that do double duty as table toppers. You'll save on stems and stave off hunger.
- *Found markets.* Strike it rich by scouring your flea market for items like birdcages and bird houses—you can talk *through* them. Also try antiques stores—not a bad place to dig up a few other vintage ideas.
- *Tea (lights) time.* Floating tea lights are making a big splash these days.

Put some food coloring in water-filled vases, and place the tea lights in those—a sure way to keep things afloat.

- *Finding forest.* We're seeing pinecones, acorns, nuts and berries—anything people might pick up from the good earth that means something special to them (spray objects metallic or gold for added flair). You're starting on a new path; take your cue from nature's endless bounty.

For more ideas on centerpiece creations—as well as how to make your own—we recommend Maria McBride-Mellinger's website (mariamcbride.com), where you can get information on and purchase any of her books, including *The Perfect Wedding* series.

THE FLOWER CHECKLIST

❑ Flower arrangements for ceremony site $_____

❑ Flower arrangements for reception site $_____

❑ Centerpieces $_____

❑ Bouquets $_____

❑ Boutonnieres $_____

❑ Corsages $_____

❑ Other flowers _____ $_____

❑ Plants for site $_____

TOTAL FLOWER COSTS $_____

Congratulations, you've figured out flowers. Now we'll master the music. . . .

Step 4.
Music

As Madonna once sang, "Music makes the people come together." Nowhere is this more true than at your wedding, where the sounds you bring in set the tone of the affair. Songs dictate when it's time for the couple to say their vows, and tell people when they should grab their partner for a spin. There's even a 1970s disco classic that lets people know it's the "Last Dance" before the party's over.

When it comes to choosing the music for your wedding, like everything else, it's up to you. You can have a twelve-piece orchestra, a hip DJ, or your brother's kazoo band. You'll probably, however, have a few questions along the way. So read on and get the facts. The two of you are about to make beautiful music together.

Standing on Ceremony

The traditional protocol for a traditional wedding in a traditional house of worship is to have music for the prelude, processional, ceremony, and recessional. Usually the church provides the organist and/or musicians, and the songs range from "The Lord's Prayer" to "Ave Maria" to anything by Mozart. Should you go this route, talk to your officiant about any changes you'd like (for instance, if secular music is allowed, can you bring in your cousin Jane to do a solo?), as well as such logistics as how long your ceremony will run so all music is coordinated with the wedding.

These days many couples who wed in a house of worship choose alternatives, such as a string quartet instead of church music or a rousing song like "Going to the Chapel" as the guests arrive. It's all up to you, but, as noted above, clear everything you want to do with the officiant. If you do hire outside professionals, make sure you go over all the details: attire, overtime fees, setup time . . . you know the drill.

Musical Chairs

The biggest musical question that couples face is whether they want a band, DJ, or both. The choice is entirely up to you, though you should keep a few considerations in mind. For one thing, your space may not be able to hold that swing band you had your hearts set on (and should this be a major issue, you'll need to book the band way ahead of time and find a space that accommodates them). Many restaurants don't have room for a lot of musicians, and don't allow DJs at all. You also need to take into consideration whether you want dancing at your reception; what used to be de rigueur is slowly changing as more couples choose small, alternative weddings with, say, one vocalist. Even if you tell guests there's no dancing, place a happening pop band in front of them and some of your tipsier attendees will more than likely get up on the tables if that's the only place they can find to boogie.

There's also the question of money. Bands will more than likely cost more than a DJ. And following this logic, the bigger the band, the heftier the price tag. You can save by hiring fewer musicians (improved sound systems these days can make up for a lot of missing instruments).

Finally, it's a question of taste: There are advantages to both bands and DJs. There's something about live music that puts people in a party spirit—think of all those concerts you went to as a kid. And if dancing's your thing, know that guests are more likely to take a spin when the orchestra launches into "Boogie Woogie Bugle Boy." With a band, there's usually not as much chatting. And, of course, a band means you can have ragtime, jazz, punk rock, or dueling banjos.

The biggest advantage of a DJ is you get to hear the songs by the artists who originally performed them—and let's face it, do you really want to hear "Oops! . . . I Did It Again" as interpreted by José's Merry Mariachi Players? DJs are a great way to go if you want a lot of audience–announcer contact. Disc jockeys are trained to work a crowd; they can also serve as master of ceremonies, announcing you as a couple, informing guests about the chain of events, and taking requests.

The best option if you're torn would be to hire both. That way, when the

SOUND BITES: MUSIC TIPS FOR BANDS AND DJS

1. *Double duty.* If you're having a cocktail hour, ask if a couple of the band members can perform. This will save you the fee of hiring a whole new group.

2. *Let's do the Locomotion?* Find out how open the DJ or band is to requests. Some professionals like to control the room; others will let you pretty much make up the playlist. Also, let them know what your policy is when someone asks for the Macarena or the Chicken Dance. If you despise these traditions, make your feelings known.

3. *Performance art.* Be clear with the people you hire how active you want them to be at your wedding. If you want the band leader or DJ to act as announcer, let him know what he'll be announcing and when. If you'd rather he remain a silent partner, say so.

4. *Who's the boss?* Always find out if the person you make the contract with is the person who'll show up at your wedding. A lot of big disc jockey organizations handle several weddings a day. You'll want to be positive that the chick who has such a seductive voice on the phone is the one who shows up.

5. *Big band business.* Go over overtime fees, how many breaks they'll need (ask if prerecorded music can be played at the break), if they'll expect to be fed, and any tipping charges. In other words, find out how much money you'll have to spend and get it in writing.

6. *How's the equipment?* You'll need to know how much time they need to set up, as well as whether they supply amps, mikes, even extension cords. If there's anything you have to provide, find out now. Also, go over space requirements and where in the room they'll set up. If they can get to your site ahead of time, that's a plus.

7. *Gridlock.* Check with the people in charge of your space to see if they can provide a backup generator. Too much power, and both the building, and you, are liable to blow a fuse. It may be a great dance tune, but the last thing *you* want to be doing is dancing in the dark.

band takes a break, the DJ can take over. Keep in mind the personalities and ages of your guests no matter whom you hire. If you've got elderly people in attendance, you want to make sure the band or DJ plays old standards. Ditto with hip tunes for the teenagers in the crowd. Yes, it's your party, but you want your friends to feel comfortable, too.

Finding Your Sound

The best way to find bands or DJs is from your friends. The style, the feel, all the elements are understood best by someone who's been there, heard that. Of course, this doesn't always work, so some good places to start for DJs are the American Disc Jockey Association (888-723-5776 or adja.org) and 1-800-Disc Jockey Online (new.800dj.com), both of which should be able to refer you to someone in your area. For bands, try the Wedding Music Information Source (weddingmusicsource.com) or the American Association of Bridal Consultants (860-355-0464), which, for a fee, can refer you to a band or DJ. Still off-key? Try college music departments, local symphony halls, even radio stations. Once you have someone in mind, it's essential that you attend a live performance. Ask the band or DJ if you can crash a party they're working, then ask for a tape to get a further taste of their sound and style.

You Should Be Dancing

If you're having a first dance, the only requirement is that the song be something close to your heart. Many couples choose the song they heard when they first met, while some go with a tune that later moved them both. Still others find a song that seems to best epitomize their romance. You should never feel obligated to pick a crowd-pleaser—it's your dance, after all. The following twenty suggestions are ideas to inspire you:

"At Last"—Etta James
"Beautiful Day"—U2
"By Your Side"—Sade
"Come Away with Me"—Norah Jones
"Evergreen"—Barbra Streisand
"Here with Me"—Dido
"Ice Cream"—Sarah McLachlan
"My Lover"—Melissa Etheridge
"Power of Two"—Indigo Girls

"The Look of Love"—Dusty Springfield

"True Colors"—Cyndi Lauper

"Unchained Melody"—The Righteous Brothers

"We've Only Just Begun"—Carpenters

"What a Wonderful World"—Louis Armstrong

"When We Collide"—k. d. lang

"Wind Beneath My Wings"—Bette Midler

"(You Make Me Feel Like) A Natural Woman"—Aretha Franklin

"Your Song"—Elton John

"You're My Best Friend"—Queen

"You've Got a Friend"—Carole King

Get Up and Boogie

Sometimes it can be so hard to think of that perfect dance song. Here, 50 classic tunes to help get your crowd on the floor. The only thing we can't help you with is deciding who leads.

"Back on the Chain Gang"—The Pretenders

"Believe"—Cher

"Boogie Oogie Oogie"—A Taste of Honey

"Brick House"—The Commodores

"Celebration"—Kool & the Gang

"Crazy in Love"—Beyoncé

"Crocodile Rock"—Elton John

"Da Ya Think I'm Sexy"—Rod Stewart

"Dance the Night Away"—Van Halen

"Dancing Queen"—ABBA

"Don't Leave Me This Way"—Thelma Houston

"Don't You Want Me"—The Human League

"Dude (Looks Like a Lady)"—Aerosmith

"No More Tears (Enough Is Enough)"—Barbra Streisand and Donna Summer

"Everyday People"—Sly and the Family Stone

"Family Affair"—Mary J. Blige

"Flashdance . . . What a Feeling"—Irene Cara

"Funkytown"—Lipps, Inc.

"Get the Party Started"—Pink

"Girls Just Want to Have Fun"—Cyndi Lauper

"Groove Is in the Heart"—Deee-Lite

"Heart of Glass"—Blondie

"Hey Ya!"—OutKast

"Hit Me With Your Best Shot"—Pat Benatar

"I Got You (I Feel Good)"—James Brown

"I Love the Nightlife"—Alicia Bridges

"I'm Coming Out"—Diana Ross

"It's Raining Men"—The Weather Girls

"I Will Survive"—Gloria Gaynor

"Lady Marmalade"—LaBelle

"Little Red Corvette"—Prince

"Love Shack"—The B-52's

"Love Will Keep Us Together"—Captain and Tennille

"Man! I Feel Like a Woman!"—Shania Twain

"Mony Mony"—Billy Idol

"Music"—Madonna

"Our Lips Are Sealed"—Go-Go's

"Relax"—Frankie Goes to Hollywood

"Respect"—Aretha Franklin

"(I Can't Get No) Satisfaction"—The Rolling Stones

"Shame"—Evelyn "Champagne" King

"Sisters Are Doin' It for Themselves"—Eurythmics

"Stayin' Alive"—The Bee Gees

"Together Again"—Janet Jackson

"Got to Be Real"—Cheryl Lynn

"Venus"—Bananarama

"We Are Family"—Sister Sledge

TIMETABLE TIP:
You should book your musical guests about eight months before the wedding—much sooner if it's a big band and you need to make sure they fit into the space. Don't put it off too much longer, unless your goal is to discover the next Nirvana and go with a local garage band.

"Y.M.C.A."—The Village People

"You Shook Me All Night Long"—AC/DC

"You Spin Me Round (Like a Record)"—Dead or Alive

THE MUSIC CHECKLIST

❏ Ceremony musicians $_____

❏ Ceremony instruments $_____

❏ Soloist $_____

❏ Reception musicians $_____

   ❏ DJ $_____

   ❏ Band $_____

   ❏ Both $_____

❏ Cocktail hour musicians $_____

TOTAL ESTIMATED COST $_____

Congratulations, you've mastered the music. Now figure out photography and videography. . . .

Step 5.
Photography/Videography

You know how much fun it is to glance through old yearbook photos to see just how silly you looked? Trust us, twenty years from now you don't want to be doing the same thing with your wedding pictures. That's why choosing a great photographer and/or videographer is such an important task. It's also one of the places you don't want to skimp on your budget. While it's tempting to take up your brother's offer to be in charge of the photos, unless he's a professional, you're better off letting him simply enjoy being a guest. Chopped-off heads and blurry close-ups are best saved for those drunken parties you'd probably rather forget anyway.

As for finding the best lens people for the job, once again, always ask recently wedded couples for recommendations, check online and in the yellow pages, and make sure to ask other vendors. We can't stress enough that, when it comes to weddings, gay or straight, it truly is a small world after all: If you've hired top-notch caterers, ask them for recommendations. Wedding pros rely on networking to survive; it's not going to be in their best interests to suggest anyone who's unfit for the job.

PHOTO FINISH: PHOTOGRAPHY TIPS AND TRENDS

- *Color your world?* Black-and-white photography has made a big comeback in wedding photography—think of that now-legendary picture of John F. Kennedy Jr. kissing Carolyn Bessette's hand. The reason: These prints are more dramatic than color. With less emphasis on the different hues, the emotion of the picture tends to take focus. Still, you didn't pick purple pansies for nothing; it's a great idea to have an even mixture of the two. Then again, if you're bored by the beginning of *The Wizard of Oz* and perk up only once Munchkinland appears, by all means be a true friend of Dorothy's and go with color.

- *Strike a pose, or strike the poses?* Another question you'll need to ponder is how many formal shots you'd like (your family lined up in front of the church) as opposed to candids (a groomsman nervously adjusting his tie). Commonly referred to as photojournalism, candid shots tend to tell more of a story, as if someone's making a documentary of your day. Formal shots are the must-haves—the cake cutting, the bouquet toss, the kiss. Most couples prefer a mixture of the two, but if you have a preference, tell the photographers you're interviewing, and ask what style they prefer. Most will have a stronger bent toward one or the other.

- *Must-see VIPs.* You want to enjoy your wedding, not spend the day making sure your photographer gets a shot of the centerpieces and the harpist you hired. During your consultation, go over a must-have list of shots (an experienced photographer should have a good idea of the kinds of pictures people want). Once the day arrives, assign a close friend or relative the task of pointing out certain individuals—Aunt Joan, your best friend from grammar school—whom you want to make sure don't get lost in the crowd.

- *Shooting schedule.* With all due respect to the tradition of not seeing the bride, or groom, before the wedding, it's becoming more popular to take photos before the ceremony. Everyone's fresh, makeup's flawless, and your guests won't have to wait at the reception while your pictures are being taken. If you want to uphold tradition, you can take photos right after the ceremony—though if you go this route, keep pictures to a minimum; you've got a party in your honor waiting to happen. While couples also opt to have the formal shots taken during the reception, this has disadvantages, too. For one thing, it means skipping out at your own party just when you're finally able to unwind. On the other hand, the fact that you *are* relaxed might come through in your photos. Remember, check your makeup and attire to make sure you're still in tip-top shape—not tipsy and disheveled.

- *The look of love.* When talking to photographers, ask to see an album of an entire wedding they shot, not just a "best of" collection. You need to understand how well they capture an entire wedding, not highlights from thirty different ceremonies.

- *Overexposure?* Ask recently wedded couples how many pictures their photographer took and if it was enough. Hint: Ninety-nine percent of the people you speak with will say they would have liked more photos. It's best to err on the side of more photographs—assuming, of course, you can afford it. Most photographers will shoot anywhere from three hundred prints (for mostly formal pictures) to up to a thousand (photojournalist shots). If you're digging too deep into your budget, place disposable cameras on the tables and designate a spot where guests can leave them at the end of your reception. You'll undoubtedly get some great candids this way, and the cost will be minimal.

- *Sure, those sweet-sixteen photos are nice, but . . .* You found a photographer: She's hip, she's hot, she's got style in spades. But the closest she's come to shooting a wedding is when she was appointed the Official Senior Prom Portrait Taker. Move on. While there are thousands of fabulous photographers in the world, as with every other aspect of your ceremony, you want someone with experience in the field. Otherwise, she might head for the railroad tracks when you tell her you'd like a shot of the train.

IN DEVELOPMENT: QUESTIONS TO ASK YOUR PHOTOGRAPHER

- Does the photographer know the space? If he's previously worked the room you're celebrating in, he's going to have a much better understanding of how to navigate it, and where the best shots should be taken.
- Are you speaking with the person who will be doing the actual photography? Sounds like a no-brainer, but if you're dealing with a larger company, the one you discuss details with may not be the one who shows up at your wedding. Make sure you meet the photographer who will take the actual prints, and get any backups (in case of emergencies) in writing.
- How will you be billed? Some photographers charge by the hour, some by the number of prints, some by a combination. If your photographer charges by the hour and you're trying to save money, see if you can hire her for two hours, rather than three.
- How many gay weddings has your photographer shot? Though it's not essential that whomever you hire has tons of experience at same-sex ceremonies, the last thing you want is someone who's squeamish about taking photos of the two men kissing. You need a photographer who's completely at ease. That doesn't mean your photographer has to be gay. Many straight photographers love to shoot gay weddings, especially because they tend to be a little less formal.
- Do you get along with your photographer? The person you hire will be a "guest" at your wedding. The better you two hit it off, the more comfort-

able you'll be around him, which will result in photographs that look more natural. You'll also probably feel a lot more relaxed letting him take a shot of you while you're applying your makeup, or trying to figure out which direction the cummerbund's pleats are supposed to go (and just so you know, they go up).

- Does your photographer know the difference between night and day? If you're having an evening ceremony, make sure the photographer's shot nighttime weddings before. The same goes if your wedding's in the daylight hours. Different times of day call for different techniques and an understanding of both natural and artificial lighting. Ignore this question, and you're liable to be left in the dark.

- Has your photographer entered the digital age? Most photographers we spoke to still prefer film to digital, claiming the quality is better. You should ask what your photographer's personal choice is, and, more important, why. Also inquire whether you can buy more prints later on, should your budget not allow for an unlimited number of photos right now.

- How is the wedding album designed? These days wedding albums can be an art unto themselves, with different-sized photos, ragged or straight edges, and love sayings attached to the portraits. Make sure you like your photographer's style—you'll no doubt be displaying this book on your coffee table for years to come. You should also be allowed to have final approval over the book. Want to create an album yourself? If you've got an artistic bent, ask if that's an option. There are also many software programs you can buy to help you if you go this route.

- Will your photographer get a great shot of the two of you? One of the differences between straight weddings and same-sex affairs is that at gay ceremonies, there tends to be less emphasis on family portraits. While that's understandable, especially if your ceremony has more friends than family, make sure your photographer knows that you want to capture the romance of the day; that means that you absolutely must have at least one fantastic shot of both of you. Twenty years from now you don't want to be looking back and saying, "Everyone seems to be having such a wonderful time. Honey, where were we?"

The Wedding Announcement Photo

If you choose to have a photo sent to your local newspaper, or simply want a portrait for family and friends, it's usually shot about two months before the wedding at the photographer's studio. Note that not all wedding photographers also shoot portraits. A good rule of thumb: Wear dark for dark backgrounds, light for light backgrounds. For lipstick enthusiasts, remember that if the photo's being shot in black and white, red lipstick will look black. Also, if you want your bouquets to be in the pictures, have your florist create mock versions of the ones you'll be holding on your wedding day. Be sure to order prints for all your family and friends at the same time, to avoid reordering costs.

The Technology of Videography

These days the question isn't always whether to have a videographer, it's whether you want two. (The advantage of duo cameras is that one can concentrate on the two of you up close and personal, while the other can capture the look of your wedding from the sidelines.) Before you turn your ceremony into a Hollywood blockbuster, however, decide if you even want a video of your day. As with every other aspect of your wedding, the choice is entirely up to you. Go over these fine-print tips before entering the video age:

- *Get rolling.* The best way to find out if a videographer is for you is to see an example of the artist's previous work. Do you like the editing? Did she capture the wedding in a way that appeals to you? If her style is what you're looking for, by all means hire her. A wedding video can offer years of endless enjoyment. Also, some videographers will let you assist in deciding on what stays in, while others will be adamant about taking care of the editing themselves. Decide how much control you need, and go from there.
- *Protecting your image.* Most videographers use a three-chip camera (which filters three primary colors into one clear, sharp signal). Also, make sure

TIMETABLE TIP:
You should scout
for photographers
and videographers
immediately after
you've picked out
your site, and have
booked them eight
months prior to the
wedding. If pho-
tographs and
video aren't a pri-
ority, and you're
not interested in
formal portraits,
you can add a
month to this
timetable. Wait
any longer and
your techie
nephew Billy prob-
ably *will* end up
being the one to
try out his new
digital camera at
your wedding.

they use wireless mikes and high-tech lighting that won't distract from the ambience of your wedding—a good videographer can shoot by candle-light.

- *What comes with the package?* Wedding videos can be straightforward images of your day, or they can include background photos, theme music, subtitles . . . pretty much anything. See how versatile the videographer is, and then be sure to let him know exactly what kind of "documentary" you'd like. Remember, you might think "The Way We Were" makes the perfect sound track for your video, until you realize seventy-five million other couples have used it as well. Let the videographer know you'd like to make original memories.

- *Space constraints.* The more untraditional your wedding locale, the more interesting your video is liable to be. There are only so many shots you can get in a house of worship (some places might forbid it altogether). If your ceremony and reception are being held in a mansion with a garden, however, there are many more location choices.

- *Director's cut.* Don't take it personally, but no one wants to see a seven-hour video of your wedding except, well, you. Learn to appreciate the art of editing and keep the video down to a reasonable time. Rule of thumb: If you need to get up to use the bathroom more than once while the video's still running, it's too long. Aim for less than two hours.

- *Now voyeurs.* Assuming you hired your photographer and videographers separately, make sure they've consulted with each other beforehand, so they know what images you'd like each of them to get, as well as how to stay out of each other's way. Generally speaking, you want all your vendors to be able to work together as a team. If they can't do that, they shouldn't be working a wedding in the first place.

- *Just say cheesy.* It's tempting to have your videographer show images of the two of you running amok in sand dunes or feeding each other cotton candy, then add illustrated Cupids shooting arrows into your hearts. But while that might sound adorable now, "cute" wears off faster than a Jessica Simpson quip. Just like those wedding photographs, make sure you're getting images you're going to be proud to look at from here to eternity. When in doubt, cut the cheese.

THE PHOTOGRAPHY/VIDEOGRAPHY CHECKLIST

❑ Wedding photographer $_____

❑ Portrait photographer $_____

❑ Extra prints for family $_____

❑ Disposable cameras $_____

❑ Videographer $_____

    ❑ One $_____

    ❑ Two $_____

ESTIMATED COST FOR PHOTOGRAPHER AND/OR VIDEOGRAPHER $_____

Congratulations, you've just conquered the world of photography/videography. Now it's time to decide on your dress code. . . .

Step 6.
Formalwear

Dresses and Gowns and Veils, Oh My!

You probably didn't see this day coming, at least not in this particular way. The fantasy, perpetuated in Hollywood and beauty magazines—and quite likely lived out in your childhood bedroom—was that someday you'd meet your handsome prince/princess, fall in love, get married, and live happily ever after. And of course, the bride would walk down the aisle in the most beautiful wedding dress on God's green earth. It's everybody's dream, right?

Not exactly. All gays and lesbians planning a wedding are looking at it from their own unique perspective (for one thing, Mr. Charming might have been replaced with *Ms.* Charming), but the one thing everyone has in common is the desire to wear something that is perfect for the occasion, and, in whatever form it takes, something that is a reflection of their love.

Whether you want to go ballroom beauty or tuxedo tomboy, we've got a look for you. (Oh, and if you're having attendants, we'll suit them up to everyone's satisfaction.)

For those of you "married" to the idea of having a unique wedding gown, this next section is for you. Remember, it takes longer to find, choose, tailor, and alter a custom-made dress than it does a pantsuit or tuxedo.

FORMALITIES, PLEASE

Billy Idol might have been onto something in the 1980s when he told us it was a "nice day for a white wedding." All dressed in black, with spiked hair and dangling crosses, the message, intended or not, was that we could have it both ways. He was right. For those of you who want to go with a traditional dress (and that number is increasing among gay women), hetero magazines are a big help in getting started. If you've ever noticed how big those tomes are, don't think it's because of endless editorial insights. Bridal publications are full of ad pages featuring every kind of dress imaginable. If you see ones you like, tear out the pages; they'll help you as you go through the maze of bridal stores.

Also, many advertisements will actually include addresses and phone numbers for stores in your region that carry the dress. Theknot.com and weddingchannel.com are two mainstream sites that provide you with "dress finders," most of which will allow you to search for gowns by designer, silhouette, sleeve length, neckline, and, perhaps most important, price. You don't buy here, but it's a great way to browse.

Where to shop? The real question is, Where don't you? In this day and age, it might be tough to find a good slice of pizza, but as for a wedding dress, you'll never walk alone. The only thing you have to decide beforehand is your budget (a wedding dress can range from a few hundred dollars to tens of thousands, so don't even think about looking at that sleeveless Vera Wang number if you've only allotted five hundred bucks). In addition, if you're a man looking to get wedded in a gorgeous gown, call ahead to make sure your favorite boutique will treat you right. For listings of gay-friendly vendors, try pridebride.com or rainbowweddingnetwork.com.

Below, a few places to start:

- *Personal best.* Couture shops carry exclusive designer dresses at, surprise, high prices. The advantage, in addition to ravishing gowns, is that you'll get a dress of high quality that is custom-made to your measurements, as opposed to one you'll have to alter. You'll also receive a lot of personal attention.

- *Miss Independent.* Independently owned bridal shops offer a variety of dresses in moderate to high price ranges. These stores either employ or work with seamstresses who fit your dress. Since you can usually find bridal accessories at these shops, the great news is that you might only have to go to one store to get the dress, shoes, and veil. And just as in a couture shop, somebody will wait on you hand and (beautifully adorned) foot.

- *Attention shoppers.* Many department stores have bridal salons as well. They don't all carry the same designers, so plan to visit a few. These salons usually provide alterations. As for accessories, it's a department store, after all. While the bridal department might have a few headpieces and veils, you'll most likely have to mall around a bit for the rest of your look.

- *The chain gang.* Very popular options these days are national bridal chains like David's Bridal. At places like this, you buy dresses off the rack from the store's label, for a fraction of the cost you'd pay in a high-end salon. These stores usually have their own alterations departments, where you'll be charged based on the work that needs to be done. Ask for an estimate first, in case you know a place that can do it cheaper.

- *Take it off.* Discount bridal outlets are another way to go. The gowns may be either from the store's label or, more likely, discontinued styles from other designers—hey, remember that fabulous dress ad you tore out of *Really, Really Modern Bride*? You might just find it here. At these stores you'll most likely buy the dress off the rack, and you'll have to find someone to do the alterations.

YOU'VE GOT THE LOOK

There are some styles you might want to consider, and you'll definitely be asked about: the ballgown, the sheath, and the A-line.

Frankly, my dears, the ballgown is the dress you've seen in every epic; think *small waist* and *huge skirt*. A sheath is a slim-fitting gown that hugs the body. An A-line looks like the letter it's named for: The seams flow vertically from the shoulders down to the skirt, which is flared.

"Figuratively" speaking, ballgowns tend to complement the small-waisted while A-lines slim you down because of their nondistinct waistlines. As for that sheath, the fabric it's made of will give you some wiggle room (thin charmeuse is made for brave hearts). Regardless, this design tends to snuggle, so whatever your figure, wear it in confidence.

TRUE COLORS (WEDDING DRESS QUESTIONS)

- How much can you alter the gown? If you see a beautiful ballgown and want to turn it into a dazzling mini, you're probably out of luck. There are only so many alterations a shop can make. If you despise one element of the dress, ask immediately if it can be changed. If not, shed a tear and move on.
- Can you wear it in the chapel? Some houses of worship have clothing restrictions—no bare shoulders, for example. Check with the officiant if you're worried your dress might be inappropriate. Remember, you can always cover shoulders with a fabulous wrap.
- Is it okay to wear white? In the first place, you've already violated any silly "rule" about what white stands for. And second, who cares? Wear whatever color you feel most comfortable in.
- When should you go dress shopping? Do yourself and your therapist a favor: Try to do all your shopping in the morning hours, or, better yet, take time off from work and go in the middle of the day. Since you'll have to make an appointment at many salons, ask if you can avoid going during rush hour.
- Can you make your own dress? Sure, and after you're finished with that task,

why don't you move on and put an end to global warming? If you're dead set on making your own gown, we're not going to stop you. Just remember, when planning a wedding you never have as much time as you think.

- Should you go with the dress the salesperson loves, even though it's three times more than you can afford? Not only should you nix the dress, you should run out of the shop. Be up front about your budget; any reputable salon will work within your price range. Also, if a salesperson says you look incredibly stunning in each outfit you try on, stun her by asking to speak with someone else.

- Should you bring your reading group to the shop for advice—or maybe the gals from the office? We suggest that you let the readers put their noses back in their books and that the gals get back on the clock. When shopping, bring one reliable friend or relative whose taste you trust. Too many opinions will only confuse you.

- Can you get a refund if you decide you don't like your dress? Unlike a martini with too much vermouth, you can't tell a salon the style of your dress is wrong and send it back. It's quite probable that your dress has been custom-ordered for you, in your size and tailored to your needs. Regardless of where you've purchased the dress, you've most likely put down a deposit. Don't expect to get it back, but do talk to the manager and see what the policy is (department stores may let you return a dress). Unlike your newfound love, however, this story usually doesn't come with a happy ending.

- Should you buy a dress in a smaller size to help you lose weight before the wedding? Buying smaller-sized clothes is a great diet motivator, but it's not advisable when you buy a wedding dress. Remember, if you do lose those extra pounds, you can always take a dress in. On the flip side, while *coming* out might have been invigorating, *taking* a dress out will be extremely costly and time-consuming.

COUNT GOWN: YOUR WEDDING-DRESS TIMETABLE

It's enough to make a drag queen not like being a girl. The dress process, from start to finish, can take four to six months. (Remember, you can go back to salons as many times as you like without putting down a deposit.) When you go to try on gowns, bring proper undergarments (strapless bra, girdle, stockings, heels, and so on) to make sure you get the best fit. Next, you need to narrow down your choices, select the gown, and begin the fittings (and there may be a lot of them). If you choose to purchase a dress off the rack or a sample from one of the salons you visit, the fittings shouldn't take too long. They're tailoring a ready-made dress to your measurements. However, if you choose a custom-made gown, leave as much time as possible for alterations and any possible problems. You'll need to order the dress between six and eight months before your wedding. Word to the size-wise: When in doubt, order the larger dress.

You should pick up your dress about three weeks before the wedding. If it has been some time since your last fitting, try on the dress before leaving the salon. Also, ask about any specific cleaning and/or handling instructions at this time so you are able to take care of the dress should a wrinkle surface or something spill on it.

DRESS ME UP: ACCESSORY OPTIONS

If you get freaked out over what veil goes with your dress, relax: The salespeople are the experts! If you can remember that the longer the dress, the longer the veil, you'll do fine. The real question, however, is whether you want to go the headgear route. Many people see the veil as an outdated symbol of virginity and, more specifically, submissiveness. Other choices are tiaras, headbands, flowers, even a hat.

As for jewels, it's all about logic: If the dress is simple, go ahead and embellish it with jewelry. If the dress is glittery enough to make Mariah Carey sing, minimize the rest of your bling. A general rule of thumb is that one meaningful piece of jewelry is always more striking than a display chest, especially if it has personal significance.

Shoes should match the formality of the dress—and remember, if you like the style but the color's wrong, you can always dye them. Equally as important, they should be comfortable. You want to look great at your wedding, and you also don't want to be running into the ladies' room every five minutes to apply another Band-Aid. Once you purchase the shoes, break them in by scuffing the soles and walking around the house in them.

DRESS FOR LESS: WHITE WEDDING OPTIONS

Because it can be a complicated process, we've devoted a lot of time to helping you find a traditional wedding dress. For those of you not going the white gown route, our task is much easier. Common choices include pantsuits (a great idea is to go with complementary, but not identical, colors). Another popular option is for one bride to wear a suit and the other, a dress. This gives the two of you a more contrasting look. And it's always chic to wear two cocktail dresses—best suited, of course, for an evening affair. Accessorize to the mini or to the max, and wear it well. All eyes will be looking at the love you share.

LET'S HEAR IT FOR THE GIRLS

Bridesmaids' dresses have come a long way, baby. Gone are the days when you'd pick out an over-the-top number in one garish color and then force, er, politely ask your attendants to wear the monstrous creations. Today's designs are fashion-forward, and, in what could possibly be considered the greatest achievement of the new millennium thus far, rewearable!

Your best bet in choosing outfits is to go with a designer you like, along with a fabric and color, and then let your attendants choose their own style within those parameters. In addition to giving your maids a say in the matter, it also allows both the small-chested and big-boned to flatter their figures in a style they find suitable. If you're set on a particular style as well as a color, you might want to let attendants choose the shade of the dress. Many designers also offer mix-and-match separates. To further help your bridesmaids personalize their outfits (and nix the 1960s airline stewardess uniform look), ask them to choose their own jewelry, or at least have them choose different pieces in a similar style.

Of course, you could always make the most daring fashion choice of all . . . skip the uniforms altogether and let them wear whatever pleases them. Or let some of them wear suits, and others go girly. Hey, they don't call a gay wedding book revolutionary for nothing!

BUSTS AND BUDGETS

One of the first questions most people have regarding bridemaids' outfits is: "Who pays?" Traditionally, your attendants are responsible for the cost, which is all the more reason for you to let them make as many choices as possible. Keep in mind, too, the different budgets of your friends—you might want to settle on something somewhere in the middle range. If you can afford it, a great gift is to pay for all, or some, of the cost. Under no circumstances are you obliged to help with payment—and by the same token, no friend should ever feel obligated to pay for an unaffordable outfit.

Start shopping about six months prior to the wedding—or even earlier if you have friends scattered around the country, because not everything will be available everywhere, particularly dresses. If you are taking charge of ordering everyone's outfits, make sure your attendants get measured by a tailor or seamstress as early as possible, and then send them the suits or gowns right away. This allows them time to try everything on and make any necessary alterations. Do this at least four to five months before the wedding. Consult with your bridesmaids, listen to their ideas, and, as God is your witness, don't ever make a bridesmaid wear orange taffeta again.

Suits, Tuxedos, and . . . Strollers?

Gay men getting married have one big plus in the fashion department: They don't have to worry about being overshadowed by the bride. And contrary to what you might think from watching *Queer Eye for the Straight Guy,* many gay men might not know much about fashion. While women tend to be more knowledgeable about formalwear, everyone wonders if he or she knows "the rules."

Guess what? You don't have to. For your wedding you can wear jeans, an aloha shirt, heck, even a Speedo if it floats your boat. On the opposite end of the spectrum, you can do your best Fred Astaire imitation and don a top hat and tails—you can also do a Ginger and wear heels. You're the boss of your own affair, and we're only here to guide you through the maze of ties, tailoring, and, of course, the tux.

MONKEY BUSINESS

For those of you going the tux route, here's a cheat sheet, so you won't feel like a baboon when the man in the shop asks if you'd like notch or shawl.

There are four main tux types:

- *Cutaway (also called morning coat).* Worn for very formal A.M. affairs, the cutaway has a long tail in back and a single button at the waist. It's usually gray or black and is worn with striped trousers and waistcoat. Rumor has it that, traditionally, it was topped off with an ascot, but since we think that particular garment has gone the way of Don Knotts on *Three's Company,* we suggest you match it up with a bow tie.
- *Stroller.* Worn when the ceremony is held before 6 P.M., the stroller varies from a tuxedo in that the coat is slightly longer, it's often another color besides black, and it's worn with pinstripes.
- *White tie.* The suit that puts the *formal* in *formalwear,* the white tie consists of solid black pants highlighted by a long black tailcoat that has no buttons, a (duh) white tie, and, most memorably, a top hat and cane. Though rare these days, they're still fashionable—nothing Marlene Dietrich wore could ever go out of style.
- *Tuxedo.* Yep, it's the garment you guys rented when you thought taking a girl to the prom would make you straight. Basically, all you need to know about tuxes is that they're not recommended unless the wedding is after 6 P.M.—this is really only a concern if you've invited Mr. Blackwell to your affair. Also, you can have a peak lapel (the name says it all), a notch (it literally looks like someone took two slices out of the collar), or, the most classic, the shawl (the collar is flat all the way around—think any James Bond flick). Even though tuxes are also called black tie, they can be worn in gray or, if you're daring, any other color you can get your hands on. Choose wisely: Remember, you're the one who gets to look at the photos for the rest of your life.

BLACK-TIE BABES

Just as guys can don dresses, girls look terrific in tuxes. And not surprisingly, if either one of you, or both, plans to go black tie, the rules are pretty much the same as for men. Simply call the formalwear store and explain the situation. If they're hesitant, or put you on hold long enough to hear an entire Celine Dion CD, hang up and call someone else. A smart store will always take your money. When you get there, the salesperson will take your measurements and guide you through the formalities of whether you want a morning coat, black tie, or any variation thereof. For both male and female couples, if your attendants are also putting on the penguin suits, you'll want them to be in a slightly different shade or style so that you stand out. One good site to turn to is pridebride.com, which helps you locate gay-owned and gay-friendly tailors in your region. It's never been so easy to be a woman in a man's world.

RENT OR STABILIZED?

Should you rent or should you buy your tux? Since a rental will cost about one to two hundred dollars and the price of a quality tuxedo can be anywhere from about five hundred to a thousand, most people rent. However, should you have the kind of job that requires you to wear a tuxedo more than two times a year, it makes sense to buy. Keep in mind that if your weight tends to fluctuate significantly, there's no tailor in the world who can keep you in the black.

SUIT YOURSELF: FORMAL ALTERNATIVES

Despite what you've probably heard over the years, it's our belief that not everyone looks good in a tux. If you're not wild over them, there are a million alternatives to try that make just as dashing a statement. A dinner jacket (which you can even buy at a vintage store and have altered) is an amazing look on anyone—plus, you won't be restricted when it comes to what you have to wear with it. Many grooms go with formal suits, usually picked out for the occasion. We've seen the (borrowed from the tropics) khakis-and-white-shirt look, which is great when accompanied with sandals. Whatever style you choose, just make sure it fits the formality of the wedding—if your guests are in black tie, and you're wearing sneakers, you might feel a little out of place. Love your look and you'll be dressed to thrill.

BASIC INSTINCTS: FORMALWEAR TIPS

- *One for all.* Rent everyone's formalwear near the site where you're having the ceremony. It's a common courtesy for formalwear shops around the country to offer free measurement services, so ask your attendants to get measured in their hometowns and give you the numbers. Once your attendants arrive, have them try on the clothes the day before the wedding, in case of any mistake in the alterations. (This goes for suits and tuxes only, obviously. Dresses are sent to attendants, as you've already read.)
- *Shoe closets.* Shoes don't come with the price of rented tuxes, and if you and/or your attendants want to save money, it's perfectly acceptable to wear your own. But do make sure they're formal and in great shape. You'll stick out like a bad blister if your soles have been unattended to.
- *Go your own way.* So Aunt Cenile knows whom to congratulate—and to show the crowd it's your day—the two of you should wear something

TIMETABLE TIP: Gowns are often the single most important element in a wedding, and, as such, something to which you want to devote enough time to get everything exactly the way you want it. Give it at least six months. You should rent tuxedos about four months before the wedding. Should your ceremony fall around a major holiday or prom season (March through June), it's advisable to take care of this six months prior to the big day.

slightly different from your attendants. It can be as simple as an alternate boutonniere or a jacket in a different shade. If you're both wearing, say, khakis, you can have all your attendants wear blue slacks. Basic rule of thumb: Mix things up a bit and ask a salesperson for guidance.

- *Stand by your (best) man.* Make sure someone close to you is responsible for collecting all the rented tuxedos and getting them back to your shop. Once again, in traditional wedding lore, this role goes to the best man. You, however, can choose anyone you like. (Things are so much more complicated at straight weddings.)

THE FORMALWEAR CHECKLIST

❑ Traditional dresses $_____

❑ Cocktail dresses $_____

❑ Suits $_____

❑ Other (vintage dresses, etc.) _____ $_____

❑ Jewelry $_____

❑ Other accessories _____ $_____

❑ Bridesmaids' dresses (if contributing) $_____

　　Tuxes

　　❑ Rented $_____

　　❑ Bought $_____

　　❑ Suits $_____

❑ Other (khakis, blazers, etc.) _____ $_____

❑ Shoes $_____

TOTAL ESTIMATED COST $_____

Congratulations, you've mastered the formalwear. Now let's get the gifts. . . .

Step 7.
Gift Registry

And you thought the gift of love was all you'd get this year. In addition to the budgeting, the endless phone calls, the who-gets-to-sit-next-to-Uncle-Armpits agony, there's another task you'll have to accomplish before the wedding. This one, however, is guaranteed to put a smile on your face and maybe a wok in your kitchen. Registering for gifts is a staple of the modern American wedding. Now that you've joined the fray, do your patriotic duty and make a wish list. Your friends and family will be thankful that you've made their shopping tasks less complicated, which is, of course, the *only* reason one registers for gifts.

Starting a gift registry early on has its advantages. Most notable is the fact that if, say, you want people to pitch in on airline tickets to Tahiti, they'll have time to save up. (Yes, in today's world, you can register for vacation packages with the assumption that it will be a joint gift.) However, if your wedding is more than a year off, either wait a bit, or keep updating your registry—items get discontinued, and you might change your mind about those monogrammed mittens you loved six months ago.

Sit down with your partner and decide what you really need. If you're already living together and your home is fully stocked, you might think outside the china pattern box. This is especially common with couples who are older and/or who've already been in serious relationships. If that's not the case, however, or if you're just beginning to make your house a home, it's a good idea to register for the basics. In addition to china, necessities include flatware, bakeware, linens, and appliances.

Most national stores offer online registries, which is a huge help, especially for friends who live far away. But keep in mind that not everyone is Internet-savvy. If possible, see if your registry list can be faxed to those who request it, or if there's a toll-free number for people to call. As for yourselves, the Inter-

THE GIFT OF GETTING: REGISTRY TIPS

1. *The price is right.* Make sure you select gifts in different price ranges, to accommodate your guests' varying budgets. It's perfectly fine to register for a washer and dryer; just be sure to also pick out that cool corkscrew everyone's been raving about.

2. *More is more.* Register for more items than you have guests. Otherwise, people will get stuck getting you something they either can't afford or simply would rather not purchase.

3. *New edition.* Keep your registry updated—check about once a month to see what's been taken. If those Chinese Fighter Fish are the only things left, you might want to think about adding that marble Chinese Checker Set.

4. *Limited edition.* Sure, it would be cool to have gifts ranging from pillowcases to pugs, but if you register at too many places, you're only going to confuse yourselves and give guests major headaches. You're better off registering at large stores that offer a big selection of items, or choosing one giant store for most items plus a small, specialty store for more unusual gifts.

5. *Cashing in.* If you'd prefer cash over gifts, have your friends and family spread the word. Note, however, that just as some people don't like to give registry items, others won't feel comfortable giving you greenbacks. It's a good idea to register someplace small (a wine shop, perhaps) to keep everyone in good spirits.

net is a great way to make your gift list without leaving your home, but, as with any purchase, you'll probably want to see it before you decide it's for you. Your best bet? Go to the store and register in person; your gifts should automatically be listed online. Many companies now offer either same-sex or nongender registries, including Tiffany & Co., Bed Bath & Beyond, Home Depot, Michael C. Fina, and Macy's.

Q & Gay: Answering Your Registry Etiquette Questions

Q: Is it okay to list your registry info on the invitations?

Gay: Think of it this way: If you were having a birthday party, would you write on the invite, "Bring me a gift!"? Nope, you'd do the sensible thing and let *everyone else* spread the word. Have people close to you let friends know where you're registered. Don't panic: People will ask.

Q: Should people bring gifts to your wedding? And if so,
do you open the presents that day?

Gay: Most people won't bring gifts to your ceremony. Your registry should include an address where packages should be sent. Still, be prepared: Some of your guests will inevitably arrive with gifts in tow. Set up an area for people to leave presents when they arrive, and do have an attendant or close friend check to make sure they're secure. As for opening them, do you really want to thank Uncle Notaste for the Chia Pet to his face? Save the unwrapping for a later date.

Q: You don't want gifts. Should you say so on the invitations?

Gay: Once again, leave this task for friends and relatives. It's important to know that some people will buy you a gift anyway—hey, there are worse things in the world. This is yet another reason to register someplace small, just in case.

Q: Your best friend from high school detention didn't send or bring a gift.
Should you spit in her face at the wedding, or hire a hit man later on?

Gay: Common wedding etiquette says that guests have up to a year after the wedding to purchase a gift, so don't assume your friend forgot or didn't care. She may be saving up, she may not have decided on the perfect present, or she simply may not have had time to shop. Fact is, most wedding gifts are purchased within two weeks of the ceremony, so give your friend a break—and not in the leg.

Q: The gifts keep coming and coming. When do you send out thank-you notes?

Gay: Ideally, you should send out thank-you notes for gifts that arrive before or on the day of the wedding within two weeks. For presents that come later on, send out cards within four weeks of the honeymoon, or the date you receive them, if after the honeymoon. And if you forget, you're not off the hook. People would much rather get a note six months after a gift—along with your apology for forgetting—than never hearing from you.

Site-Specific: Online Registries We Like

Theknot.com. Though not a "gay" site, the company is extremely gay-friendly and has a great online registry, with categories like Barbecue Equipment and Camping Gear. For the moneybags among you, you can even register for a BMW Roadster. Theknot.com also offers a Create-a-Gift program, which lets you register for unique gifts—ballroom-dancing lessons, a weekend trip to the country—by figuring out how much the specific gift will cost, then requesting that guests purchase American Express gift checks that can be used toward the present.

Weddingchannel.com. Again, not specifically for gay couples, but it's a well-organized site with high-end retailers, such as Pottery Barn, Fortunoff, and Tiffany & Co.

Rainbowweddingnetwork.com. This site includes only gay-owned and -friendly vendors. Included are sites that offer hardware, electronics, linens, pottery, china, and furniture, to name but a few. Couples link to the sites promoted, note the item number and description of merchandise, and bring the information back to their registry at the main site.

The Presents of Your Presence

The reality is, weddings are very expensive events for everyone involved, some more so than others. If you sense that a guest's finances are going to make gift buying difficult, think about discreetly asking him if he could do a reading, make sure the flowers get delivered to the correct addresses, even help bartend. You don't need to phrase your request as an "I know you can't afford to buy us something" scenario. Simply tell the person that you could use someone to make sure everyone signs the guest book, and if he could do that, it would be the best possible gift he could give.

THE WEDDING-GIFT CHECKLIST

Since this is one area that doesn't involve you doling out dollars (phew!), we've made a list of some of the more basic items you should think about registering for.

FORMAL TABLEWARE
- ❏ China
- ❏ Crystal
- ❏ Silverware

EVERYDAY TABLEWARE
- ❏ Dishes
- ❏ Glassware
- ❏ Flatware

COOKWARE
- ❏ Pots and pans
- ❏ Coffeemaker
- ❏ Blender
- ❏ Microwave
- ❏ Toaster
- ❏ Food processor
- ❏ Other _____

BEDDING
- ❏ Sheets
- ❏ Pillows and pillowcases
- ❏ Pillow shams
- ❏ Blankets
- ❏ Comforter
- ❏ Duvet
- ❏ Bed skirt

BATH
- ❏ Hand, face, and bath towels
- ❏ Guest face, hand, and bath towels
- ❏ Shower curtain
- ❏ Bath mat

ELECTRONICS
- ❏ Television
- ❏ DVD player
- ❏ VCR
- ❏ Stereo system
- ❏ Computer
- ❏ Personal digital assistant
- ❏ Digital camera
- ❏ Camcorder
- ❏ MP3
- ❏ Other _____

MISCELLANEOUS
- ❏ Furniture
- ❏ Gardening equipment
- ❏ Camping gear
- ❏ Outdoor dining (grill, tables, chairs, etc.)
- ❏ Travel
- ❏ Other _____

Congratulations, you've gotten through gifts. Now we'll go wrap up the rings. . . .

Step 8.
Rings

Considering the fact that three of the top-grossing movies in history are all about a ring, it's a safe bet to say that people are big on bands. Gold or silver, diamond or dime store, rings are a wedding staple. Unlike the case of heterosexual unions, however, rings don't often play much of a starring role at gay weddings. For one thing, two men aren't particularly inclined to purchase engagement rings. Perhaps to break free of male-female roles, or to symbolize equality in the relationship, it's not all that common for gay women to buy them, either. But never fear, queers, there are no rules or regulations in this department; many girls still want engagement rings (did you see the rock on Melissa Etheridge's babe?), and some guys go gaga for diamond-studded bands of gold.

Whatever your position on the ring cycle, familiarize yourselves with a few important details, decide which way you want to go, and start searching. Soon you, too, can be lords—and ladies—of the rings.

Soft Rocks and Heavy Metals

Before you buy that diamond dazzler you saw in the window of Rings R Us, you should learn basic ring facts, as well as how to make sure you don't run into a ring sting. First, get to know the diamond details, commonly referred to as the 4 Cs: carat, color, clarity, and cut.

These four elements are essential to understand because they determine the quality of your ring. Also, each person will have a different priority when choosing the right ring. For some, color is more important (a colorless ring is the most valuable), while for others that carat size says it all. But don't be fooled—*carat size* actually refers to the weight of the ring, as opposed to the size of the rock.

To learn more about the 4 Cs—as well as contact information for reputable dealers in your area—log on to jewelers.org. This is the official website for the Jewelers of America, a national association that guarantees ethical practices among its members.

While you're polishing up on Diamonds 101, here's some practical information on metals:

- *Silver.* This is your cheapest option. Sterling-silver jewelry is 92.5 percent pure silver (alloy metals are added to give this soft metal durability) and will be identified as such.
- *Gold.* Pure gold is twenty-four-karat, but, like silver, alloys are added to strengthen this metal. The most commonly used gold in the United States is fourteen-karat (58.5 percent gold). If it's in your budget, stay above ten-karat gold. Also, you can find gold in different colors, including white, green, rose, and, yes, pink (and they say they don't make gold with gays in mind).
- *Platinum.* It's one of the most durable metals. Not surprisingly, it's also one of the most expensive. Platinum is heavier and purer than gold; it's also hypoallergenic.

Circle Jerks: A Few Ring Things to Beware

Be wary of stores that advertise jewelry sales. Often the "sticker" price is inflated to make you think you're getting a deal, when in actuality you're paying the retail price.

Make sure the cost of your ring includes both the setting and the diamond. Yep, like those amazing sweepstakes vacation "prizes" that don't include airfare, some retailers will advertise the price of the ring setting, diamond not included.

Finally, make sure you buy from an accredited jeweler. As appealing as it might be to purchase your ring from that shack on Route 77, it's a bad idea.

Twenty years from now you don't want to find out you're *wearing* glass, instead of something that can cut it.

TIMETABLE TIP:
Like everything else, the earlier the rings are taken care of, the better. Although six months before the wedding is preferable, you can get away with ordering your rings four months prior.

Rock and a Hard Place

In 2000 a United Nations investigation reported that Angola's rebel National Union for the Total Independence of Angola raised several million dollars to purchase weapons through the sale of diamonds. Since other countries have had similar problems (most notably Sierra Leone), many couples forgo diamond rings altogether. Although the chances of buying an illegal diamond are slim, if you'd rather not risk it, avoid the rocks. You'll save money, and you may even be helping to eliminate the spread of war.

Diamonds Aren't Forever

Want a rock but lack the cash? Consider a hand-me-down ring from Uncle Art or Aunt Sophie. You can always get it resized. Another idea: Make your ring as alternative as your wedding. Try other gems or semiprecious gems—birth signs are a wonderful, and sentimental, option—and set it in gold. To make the rings more special, get them engraved. Like everything else at your wedding, nothing is set in stone.

THE RINGS CHECKLIST

❑ Engagement ring $_____

Wedding bands

   ❑ Silver $_____

   ❑ Gold $_____

   ❑ Platinum $_____

   ❑ Other _____ $_____

❑ Resizing fee $_____

❑ Alterations $_____

❑ Alternate stones $_____

❑ Engraving $_____

TOTAL ESTIMATED COST $_____

Congratulations, you've mastered the rings. Now go triumph over transportation . . .

Step 9.
Transportation

As everyone knows, you've got to get to the church (or synagogue, or mosque, or Cinderella's Castle) on time. What you might not know is the best—and smartest—way to get there in style. Whereas some couples have their hearts set on stretch limos, others would rather show up in a beat-up old Volkswagen or matching Harleys. Your mode of transportation is as individual as you are. But to make sure you don't have a Rhoda-on-the-subway moment, read on for hot wheels and cool deals.

To find your vehicle, ask vendors (caterers or site managers are a good place to start) for referrals, check out those good old-fashioned yellow pages, or log on to www.limo.org for recommendations in your area. WeddingChannel.com has a service for searching and comparing limousine quotes, based on the dates you need the service, your vehicle preference, and number of passengers. All set? Start your engines and get ready to drive off into the sunset together.

Freeway of Love

Here's the traditional transportation procedure. The bride arrives with her father and attendants in a limousine paid for by her family (in addition to any parking expenses) and arranged by the groom. The groom's parents pick up the cost of the groom's and the best man's transportation.

If you want to take on male-female roles, by all means go this route. However, most of you will probably want to try something a little different. Your transportation options include stretch limos, town cars, trolley cars, your own car, luxury cars, motorcycles or mopeds, even horse-drawn carriages.

Stretch limos are still probably the most popular option for all weddings, but with prices ranging from three hundred to five hundred dollars for a four-hour period, this may break your budget. To save, consider a color other than white, black, or silver—remember that maroon Barbie Corvette you loved as a kid? A color like that could easily lower the price. Whichever way you go, ask about special features and what the additional cost is. Pick the ones you like (champagne, perhaps), nix the ones you can do without (maybe the sunroof), and definitely get rid of the ones you'll never use (if you plan on watching TV on the way to the wedding, you've got other prime-time issues).

Going down a notch, the national average for a regular limousine or a town car is about fifty dollars an hour (always inquire about how many hours the price includes, and ask if that's a minimum or if you can drop the time down a bit). You'll still save a bundle if you rent a car (plus, you'll have it for a whole day), so if your mode of transportation's not that important, you'll find Hertz quite painless.

Carpooling

Before you make arrangements, take a head count of how many people you're going to provide transportation for. Stretch limos generally hold ten to twelve passengers, regular limos hold four to six, town cars hold two to four, and vans can usually carry about seven people. If you are shuttling people between the ceremony and the reception, make like the Partridge Family and opt for a bus, which holds up to fifty-two people.

RIDE LIKE THE WIND: TRANSPORTATION TIPS

- *Stall and deliver.* Make sure the driver has all the pickup times and correct addresses. Get a backup driver's name in case of emergency, and always exchange cell phone numbers in case there are any questions on either end.
- *Cool runnings.* Find out what your driver's attire will be, and request any changes if necessary.
- *Vehicle extras.* You'll probably be expected to tip your driver. Find out what the rate is, and assign someone to take care of the bill. Be sure to check if the company pays for the gas or if you're expected to pump up the cash.
- *Key exchange.* If you'd like to have valet service, plan on five attendants per hundred guests at twenty to twenty-five dollars per. If you prefer nonvalet attendants (these people direct traffic and staff the parking area), count on three to four per hundred guests for the same price.
- *Thorough fares.* Check on any group discounts if you rent more than one vehicle. If the money's no different, they may provide extra amenities, such as free champagne.
- *Flights of fancy.* You're not responsible for providing transportation for any guests flying to your wedding. Still, you should make their trip as easy as

TIMETABLE TIP: Transportation planning can wait up to about three months before the wedding. However, if you're booking limos and your wedding falls during prom time or graduation season (March through June), make arrangements five to six months in advance.

possible by providing detailed maps to your site and contact numbers in case they get lost.

- *Backing up.* Always have a backup plan if something goes wrong and you have no transportation to your wedding. It's much nicer to show up to the ceremony on time and in Dad's pickup than to phone your vows in.

THE TRANSPORTATION CHECKLIST

❏ Cars

    ❏ Stretch limo(s) $_____

    ❏ Limo(s) $_____

    ❏ Town car(s) $_____

    ❏ Rental car(s) $_____

    ❏ Taxi(s) $_____

    ❏ Bus(es) $_____

    ❏ Other _____ $_____

❏ Valet $_____

❏ Parking fees $_____

TOTAL ESTIMATED COST $_____

Congratulations, you've mastered transportation. Now we're off to imagine invitations. . . .

Step 10.
Invitations

And the envelope, please . . . There's something truly special about receiving personal notes in the mail (provided it's not that final-notice "love letter" from the electric company). Since the advent of e-mails and faxes, it's also quite rare. Telegrams don't arrive anymore to congratulate you on your new job, and scribbled-out teen gossip from pen pals has gone the way of Shaun Cassidy. The wedding invite just might be the last Great American Letter, the end of an era that started with the pony express and is finishing up with the announcement of your wedding celebration.

Your loved ones will be as thrilled to receive invitations as you are to send them. You want each invite to provide all the pertinent information (giving out the wrong date could put a damper on things), and they should be beautiful. The wedding invitations should indicate the style of your wedding—a Halloween bash probably won't mesh with Tiffany-blue paper—and, most of all, they should reflect the two of you.

Before Hand

Don't pull out your favorite ballpoint just yet. First, make sure you've finalized your guest list. The two of you should check (and double-check) who made the final cut, so to speak, so you don't accidentally send off a note to Aunt Julie, only to have to seat her in the kitchen with a bowl of spaghetti when she shows up unexpectedly. Also, go over space constraints: If you're having your ceremony in a room that comfortably seats fifty, don't invite seventy-five guests on the hunch that a third of them won't show—you may be more popular than you think.

You should also have gotten the correct addresses of everyone you're inviting immediately. And since people do move, make sure you've updated that date book. You'll save money if you take care of the invitations all at once. Additional orders and rush jobs will cost extra.

The Price Is Right

Next on your list is figuring out how much money you want to spend. Much of this will depend on how elaborate you'd like your cards to be, but also keep in mind that, in addition to thank-you notes, you might have save-the-date cards, response cards, reception cards, and, of course, that infamous piece of tissue paper that, like Cher, will rightfully be there for all time despite the fact that no one quite knows why.

To help you get started, check out weddingchannel.com, which has an invitations budget sheet that you can download. If you're computer-savvy, look into purchasing a software program that can help you make your own invitations. You should also decide whether you want to go with a local stationer for personal (and more expensive) attention, or choose a department store, large stationery retailer, or website to order. (In the mainstream, try theknot.com; if you want a gay grip, go to pridebride.com.)

It's All Inside: What Invites Include

In addition to the actual invitation, here's a quick reference guide to what may or may not be included in your wedding invitation:

- *The first envelope.* It's simply the envelope inside the envelope that holds the actual invitation. This envelope has the guest's name and address, as well as your return address.
- *Reception card.* The card that tells people where your reception will be held. If you're having your ceremony and reception at the same location, you don't need to include this.
- *Response card.* The response card is a separate note (including a self-addressed, stamped envelope) asking guests to indicate their intentions to attend. Some people use response cards to offer guests a choice of entrée for the main meal.

In addition to the above, people include maps, hotel information, rain locations, and pretty much anything else they deem important. Keep it to a minimum; remember, you have to pay the postage for any extras.

And finally, a "note" about save-the-date cards. These cards, mailed separately from your invitation, should be sent if you're having your wedding over a holiday weekend or in a faraway place. They should be sent immediately after you've set the date, and should include the date, city, and state of the wedding, in addition to any phone numbers for hotels you recommend.

And Now for Something Completely Traditional

In the straight wedding world (you remember that place: It existed before chapter 1), invitations list the proper names of the people hosting the wedding (usually the parents of the bride) first, followed by the bride's first and middle names. Her last name is included if the groom's parents are helping with finances or are the sole hosts. The date is written out next, followed by the wedding site, city, and state. If both sets of parents are hosting, the bride's parents' names are listed first. If the couple is hosting, the first line includes the invitation request (for example, "The honor of your presence is requested by Joe and Suzie . . ."). If everyone's pitching in, the bride's and groom's respective full names are listed along with both sets of parents (bride first).

Back in homo land, you can certainly use the above as guidelines, but chances are there will be dissimilarities. List as hosts anyone who is pitching in, followed by the wedding information—the word *honour* spelled with a *u* signifies that it's a religious ceremony. As discussed earlier, if you are the sole hosts, list your names alphabetically, or by any other satisfactory manner. Just don't fret about it too long.

Handmade in America

These days, computers can do just about anything—save choosing whether you should go with buttercream or fondant icing—so many couples are mak-

TIMETABLE TIP:
Order stationery
about six months
ahead of time, so
invitations will be
ready to go two
months before the
big day. Give
guests approxi-
mately a month
to RSVP.

ing their own invitations. Various types of card stock are available at station-ers, art stores, and office supply establishments. There are many software pro-grams you can buy, and some fonts can be downloaded on the Internet. Sealing wax can be used to close homemade invitations. PrintingPress Pro software (available at mountaincow.com) is a great program for creating invi-tations and announcements. We also like weddingsoft.com and ed-it.com. (Always make sure any program is compatible with your operating system be-fore you buy.)

If you're a PC user, check to see if you have Microsoft Publisher on your computer. This program offers templates and clip art that would be useful for invitation making. Mac users should look to see if they have PageMaker, Illustrator, QuarkXPress, or Photoshop on their system. Also, if you are going to print at home, use a laser printer. You don't want to spend time and money creating a masterpiece that will look mediocre because of your printer's quality.

SEND YOUR LOVE: INVITE TIPS

- *Extra, extra!* Once you've picked out the invitations, order twenty to twenty-five extra, as well as additional envelopes. This will not only allow for mistakes, but also leave you with a few as keepsakes. And be sure to in-clude in your count invitations for guests you might invite later.
- *It's a date.* Get the date that the printed invites will be sent to you. You want to make sure you have enough time before you have to send them out.
- *All the trimmings.* If you're planning on hiring a calligrapher, do so about four months before your wedding. Hand-printed envelopes can cost as much as two dollars each. That's not too bad if you're expecting forty guests, but if you have two hundred people coming . . . well, you do the math. Engraved invitations (the words are raised above the paper) look beautiful, but can be very expensive. It's better to have flat letters than a bumpy budget.
- *RSVWho?* As soon as replies come in, make a chart and check off names. (It will give you practice for all those thank-you notes you get to write.)

- *Give me proof.* Proofread all names, addresses, and dates before invitations are printed. When your order is ready, proof them again. It may sound tedious, but do you really think Ms. k. d. langge is going to be thrilled about getting that invite?
- *Do It Yourself.* Like any important documents, take all your invitations to the post office yourself. Don't drop them in a mailbox.
- *Mr. Postman.* Finally, make sure to take an invitation with all enclosures to the post office to have it weighed for proper postage. The last thing you need is to receive two hundred wedding invitations in the mail—all of them your own.

THE INVITATION CHECKLIST

❑ Invitations $_____

❑ Thank-you notes $_____

❑ Reception cards $_____

❑ Response cards $_____

❑ Save-the-date cards $_____

❑ Other (maps, rain cards, calligraphy, engraved lettering, etc.) _____
$_____

❑ Software programs $_____

❑ Postage $_____

TOTAL ESTIMATED COST $_____

Congratulations, you've just mastered the invitations. Now we continue to understand announcements. . . .

Step 11.
Announcements

And you were wondering why we kept a whole step open for announcements.

The traditional "announcement" is the wedding-day card you send to those people you're not actually inviting to the ceremony—friends, colleagues, rich old relatives. The wording is very similar to the wedding invitation, and people will often send gifts. The main difference, then, between a wedding invitation and a wedding announcement is that, with an announcement, you're telling people your wonderful news, and while not invited, you'll gladfully accept a gift.

How very nice for you.

We here at *Gay and Lesbian Weddings* are out, loud, and proud about a whole new approach to the announcement genre: namely, the history-in-the-making decision by major newspapers across the country to include same-sex couples in their wedding pages (with a photo, natch!). Smaller newspapers like the Minneapolis *Star Tribune* were the first to jump on the bandwagon, but the earth seemed to move when the *New York Times* published its first-ever gay wedding announcement on September 1, 2002.

As of March 2004, 245 papers across the country have joined the club (for a complete list, go to www.glaad.org). If you read any of these publications, nary a Sunday goes by that you don't see a smiling male-male or female-female couple proudly telling the world about their backgrounds, their jobs, and, most important, their official commitment to each other.

If you'd like your announcement in the paper, call the style or lifestyle editor about four months before your wedding and ask what the procedure is. You'll most likely have to send in a black-and-white photo, and each paper has specific guidelines (for instance, the *New York Times* asks that, in the photo, you try to make your eyebrows align). Then, shortly before your wedding day, pick up that style section, grab a cup of joe, or Joe or Josephine, sit back, and look for your announcement. The only real difference between your blurb and the other ones on the page? Directionals next to your (same-sex) names.

By the way, just so they don't feel excluded, please remind all your straight friends that they, too, are allowed to participate in this wonderful expression of love.

We'll see you in the papers!

———

Total estimated cost? The price of your smile!

Step 12.
Grooming

Now it's your turn. You've bonded with bakers, made friends with florists, even patched up that feud between your partner and her parents. The wedding's just days away, and you're going to be the belle (or beau) of the ball. That means you'll get your eyebrows waxed, schedule a facial, maybe even try one of those fancy-schmancy seaweed wraps—and that's before you bronze!

So all you need to do next is pick up that phone and start punching numbers, right? Wrong.

While beauty may only be skin deep, getting to the surface requires a lot of digging around. To make sure you don't get stuck in the mud pack, we've listed important time lines, hairdos—and don'ts—and offered up some last-minute wedding-day tips. Read on for flawless coverage.

Hair Apparent

For those of you with long or longish hair, if you have a favorite hairstylist, don't wait until the last minute to book him. Make an appointment at least six weeks in advance, and be sure to tell him you're having a wedding. Tell him about any hairstyles you're considering, and listen to his opinions. A good stylist will tell you that, for your wedding, you should look like yourself, only better. That means no drastic cuts or changes—if you've never tried an Afro, now's probably not the best time to experiment. If you'd like a major overhaul (say, you've decided to finally try short hair after years of wearing it long), make the first cut at least six months before your wedding. That way, if you despise the look, you've got plenty of time to let it grow back.

For those of you with short dos, get your hair cut about a week before the wedding—you'll want it to grow out a little. If you'd like to do something drastically different (changing the color, nixing the ponytail), give yourself six months' leeway in case the look backfires. Even getting rid of the gray is something you want to try a few times before the wedding, especially if you're doing it yourself. If you've suddenly decided a mustache is just the thing to make you look macho, here's a good rule of thumb: If you haven't started growing it by the time you've picked up this book, leave the look to Tom Selleck and let your lips speak for themselves.

Makeup Test

It's a lot less common for people to have a good makeup artist on hand than it is a hairdresser. For wedding-day makeup, ask friends for referrals, and check out department store cosmetics counters and spas to see what kinds of services they offer. (Some places have artists-in-training who will cost you a lot less than the woman who handles George Hamilton when he's in town.) Even if you're not nuts about makeup, keep in mind that without at least a touch, you're more than likely to look washed-out in photographs.

Putting It Together

Whether or not you book wedding-day hair and makeup stylists is, of course, up to you. If you can afford only one, it's probably best to go with the guy with the blow dryer. Many people feel secure enough to do their own makeup; some prefer it. A do-it-yourself Evita chignon, however, is liable to leave you crying.

If you are booking hair and/or makeup just for yourself, allow about forty-five minutes for each artist, and factor in their travel time. (Generally, hair is done first so your face stays fresh longer.) If you are making a morning of it with your wedding attendants, make sure you either have extra time for all of them, or hire additional artists. Generally, stylists charge by the hour, so bringing in more of them doesn't necessarily mean going overbudget—they'll be finished sooner.

With both hair and makeup artists, do a trial run a couple of weeks before the wedding to make sure they've captured the look you want and that you're not allergic to any products they use.

Waxing Sentimental

For women and men, if you get your eyebrows waxed regularly, continue your usual routine, and schedule an appointment a week before the wedding. If you're comfortable with that Frida Kahlo unibrow but want to wax off before the ceremony, do it a few weeks beforehand. For first-timers, you're likely to experience raw or broken-out skin.

As for the honeymoon, if you're removing anything south of the border, the same rule applies. Thinking about a Brazilian? Seek the services of an esthetician trained in this technique. A proper waxing should leave you hair-free for about a month, so you should have plenty of legroom. Speaking of which, you guys who want smooth sailing anywhere on your bod should call ahead to make sure the aesthetician is comfortable treating men.

Finally, you should never wax if you are using Retin-A or any other acne treatments; these will often make skin supersensitive.

GIRLS IN VOGUE AND VANITY FAIRIES: LAST-MINUTE TIPS

- *Keeping face.* If you're going to treat yourself to a facial, make sure you schedule it about three weeks before the wedding. Facials draw out impurities in the skin, which can lead to mild breakouts.
- *Finger tips.* You should schedule that manicure the day before the wedding. You run the risk of smudges if you wait till the day of.
- *The white stuff.* You don't have to spend a fortune for whiter teeth. Plenty

of over-the-counter products can help brighten your smile. Most take at least a week's worth of application, so plan ahead. Some inexpensive and effective products include Crest Whitestrips Premium, Rembrandt 2-Hour White, and the BriteSmile To Go pen.

- *Foot patrol.* Heck, you could probably make a pedicure appointment a couple of hours before your ceremony. Chances are, however, that you're going to be on your feet the day of your wedding. Pamper those pedals a few days prior. Better yet, schedule a manicure/pedicure at the same time. You'll probably even save money with a package deal.

- *The naked truth.* If you've got the time, do yourself a favor and book a massage the day before the wedding—this is also when you should treat any stressed-out friends and relatives. The hours lost will be made up for by all those relaxed nerves.

- *And just for the record . . .* In the weeks leading up to the wedding, drink lots of water and keep your diet full of fruits and vegetables. This combination will provide you with antioxidants, flush out toxins, and help keep your skin clear for the big day. Avoid caffeine as much as possible, and keep the drinking to a minimum. They both dry out your skin and often increase your anxiety. Try to stay on your regular sleeping schedule, take time out every day for some sort of exercise (a short, brisk walk can do wonders for stress), and periodically remind your partner of your love. Then go ahead and make your day.

THE GROOMING CHECKLIST

❑ Hairstylist $_____

❑ Makeup artist $_____

❑ Hairstylists for attendants $_____

❑ Makeup artists for attendants $_____

❑ Eyebrow waxing $_____

❑ Body waxing $_____

❑ Facial $_____

❑ Teeth whitening $_____

❑ Manicure $_____

❑ Pedicure $_____

❑ Massage $_____

❑ Other comforts _____ $_____

TOTAL ESTIMATED COST $_____

Congratulations: You've just mastered the 12-Step Wedding Planner. Now let go and let love . . .

CREATIVE
WEDDING
IDEAS

Garth & Ray

WHO: Garth Kobl, thirty-eight, and Ray Rigdon, forty-six, after a twenty-year courtship.

WHEN: Saturday, July 5, 2003.

WHERE: Grace Church Van Vorst, Jersey City, New Jersey. One hundred and ten guests for a five o'clock church wedding; outdoor reception immediately following at Joe's Bar, Jersey City. The catered buffet dinner had a Middle Eastern theme.

THE WAY THEY WORE: Rented tuxes.

NOTICEABLY ABSENT: Attendants.

WHY THEY WON'T BE THANKING ANYONE FOR THE CERAMIC DALMATIAN: The couple registered with gift-certificate accounts at ABC Carpet and Home and J&R Music World.

ENTERTAINMENT TONIGHT: Three rock bands performed. The metal act Made Out of Babies was the evening's finale.

WALK THIS WAY: The woman who introduced them in 1983 walked Garth down the aisle. They hadn't seen her in eighteen years.

KEEPING THEIR RELIGION: An Episcopalian minister officiated. She also gave them premarital counseling.

HOLY WHOOPS! She pronounced them "husband and wife" before stopping to correct herself.

WHAT THEY OVERCAME: When the identical rings were handed to the minister, she had no idea which one was for whom. The jeweler (a friend) ran up from his seat to tell her.

MAKEOVER TIPS: "We shouldn't have waited until the last minute to rent the tuxes," says Garth. "I hated my bow tie, and ended up wearing a bolo."

WHY A WEDDING PLANNER WOULD HAVE HELPED: They rented the tuxes in question two weeks before the Big Day.

HONEYMOON G-SPOT: Ten days in Florida with Ray's family.

PARTING WORDS: "There are people I know who are on their second divorce," Garth says. "They have no respect for the institution of marriage. After twenty years together, we thought a celebration of our lifelong commitment was appropriate." Adds Ray, "At one point I looked at the crowd and realized we'd been together longer than anyone we'd invited."

The wedding has left the building. Now that we've covered the linguistics of your ceremony, it's time to get a little playful. Like you and your partner, weddings come in all shapes and sizes, and there's no rule that says you have to play it straight—it's a little too late for that anyway. Alternative wedding ideas have been around as long as alternative wedding couples, and, as that latter group rises in number, so does the idea of making your ceremony slightly different from the one *someone's* mom used to make. While for years heterosexual couples have been doing the Disney theme or letting Elvis officiate, gay couples are celebrating with Halloween bashes (orange and black, really), skydiving's-the-limit ceremonies, and tropical-island affairs. Think about inviting your guests for a "long-weekend wedding," or hire a mariachi band! You could be daring and spontaneous and make yourselves a "surprise wedding" (but you'd have to forget about the gift getting). This is your time in the spotlight, so if an alternative wedding is what you want, go all out and do it your way. And if you can't help falling in love in Vegas, relax: Elvis is now available for same-sex ceremonies.

THE LONG-WEEKEND WEDDING

This trend is making major waves for both straight and gay couples. For a long-weekend wedding, plan your ceremony around a holiday—say, Memorial Day weekend—and turn the ceremony into a three-day party. Typically, on Friday night guests who aren't invited to the rehearsal dinner are given a detailed list of options in the area—cool bars, hot coffeehouses. On the day of the wedding, there's often some kind of group event (softball games are common; so's bowling), leaving time for everyone to get cleaned up before the main event. Sunday is good for a casual brunch or lunch affair. If you really want to stretch out the weekend, and spend as much time with your loved ones as possible, add something like theater or opera tickets, a nighttime beach bonfire (check with park officials first), or an old-fashioned game of Truth or Dare—best suited for friends who've known one another a long, long time.

THE LONG-DISTANCE WEDDING

Often confused with the above, long-distance weddings require you to pack up and bring your entire ceremony to a faraway locale. Although the idea of having a ceremony in the Caribbean might seem far too extravagant, as well as homo-impossible, it doesn't have to be either. Financially speaking, you can actually save money: First, you're limited in terms of the number of guests you can invite. Some people won't be able to take the time off, and some just won't want to travel. (Don't plan this type of affair if you're planning a large guest list.) The other financial plus is that, at many destinations, one coordinator takes care of everything, from the cakes to the catering. And those expensive flowers? In a tropical setting, luscious foliage is already there.

Long-distance weddings are increasingly popular, and resorts are starting to open up to the gay market. Many of the websites listed in Resources can help direct you to a gay-friendly locale. Another advantage to a long-distance wedding in a gorgeous spot is that you don't have to travel any farther for the honeymoon.

THE SURPRISE WEDDING

No, it's not you who is getting the surprise of your life . . . but your friends will! At this type of affair, invite as many guests as you'd like to what's billed as your engagement party, or, if you want to get really sneaky, some other event such as a birthday, the anniversary of when you met—this ensures that you have your closest friends with you. At some point during the evening, someone makes the announcement that the two of you are tying the knot, and (surprise!) it turns into a wedding. You'll have to forgo some of the traditional ceremony aspects—guests will probably be tipped off if your "party" is being held in a church—but you'll also be relieved of some prep work—toss out that seating chart now! One big plus? Since weddings are stressful for everyone, including the guests, a surprise wedding means everyone will arrive relaxed and ready to have a great time.

"No, it's not you who is getting the surprise of your life . . . but your friends will!"

Different Strokes: Other Themes That Are Coming Out

It's a small gay wedding world after all. For any of the wedding themes listed below, it's amazing how many companies and hotels are receptive to gay couples who want to wed their own way.

- *Scuba wedding.* If it's a sea of love you're after, try saying (*try* being the operative word here) your vows underwater. Dive resorts all over the Caribbean are finding this an increasingly popular way to wed. Ask the concierge if your resort has someone who can officiate; if not, have an ordained friend put his sea legs to good use.
- *Nude beach wedding.* All you really need is a clothing-optional beach, a permit for food and drink, and a lot of guests willing to throw caution—and everything else—to the wind. One Caribbean five-star hotel owner we know (who spoke on the condition that we not, um, bare his name) will gladly officiate on his resort's private nude beach. Now *that's* personal service!
- *Celebrity wedding.* Everyone dresses up as his or her favorite celebrity (though the couple of the moment gets first diva rights). A variation is to

have just the two of you get ready for your movie star close-up, and play "Celebrity," in which the name of a famous figure is taped on each guest's back. The "celebrities" then have to ask yes-or-no questions until they figure out who they are. This is a popular party ice-breaker for nonweddings, too.

- *Western wedding.* Adapted from the straight world (isn't it usually the other way around?), though its gay metamorphosis is understandable. Guests dress in full-fledged cowboy gear—yep, that means chaps and stirrups, hats and belt buckles. Popular sites include corner bars (with western-stocked jukeboxes), backyards, and barns (if you can find one). Beer is the main drink, but those hearty shots of tequila add a nice jolt. Ah, shoot, it's just a great way to rope your partner in.
- *Sky diving wedding.* Shout out your love from the skies (and good luck finding a willing bridal party). This is the only wedding we know of where the phrase *I felt like I was walking on air* makes complete sense.
- *Winter wonderland wedding.* Talk about a fairy tale: At New York's legendary Tavern on the Green restaurant in Central Park, you can ride a horse-drawn carriage to the site (snow courtesy of Mother Nature), where the restaurant will gladly throw you the gay wedding of your dreams in one of six private rooms (or in the gardens for a Summer of Love theme). Call 212-873-4111 or go to tavernonthegreen.com for more information.
- *Elvis wedding.* Yep, even the King will croon for the queens. The Chapel of Las Vegas caters exclusively to gay and lesbian couples, with an Elvis impersonator belting out hits—unless, of course, you'd prefer a disco or beach party theme. Call 800-574-4450 or visit gaychapeloflasvegas.com.
- *The storm-San-Francisco's-courthouse-and-get-married-on-the-spot wedding.* Over four thousand couples can't be wrong. Here's hoping this idea catches on everywhere!

Home Grown: Adding Culture to Your Wedding

He's Cuban and you're Italian, and you both want to include something from your heritage in the ceremony. Can you combine separate cultural elements without turning the wedding into a gay version of *West Side Story*? Certainly. In this case, a great idea would be to make mojitos the signature drink and have a pasta dish as one of the main courses. Whatever your ethnicity or religion, there's always a way to personalize your wedding. Here are just a few sample ideas to mix or match. Whatever you decide, you'll end up as "one."

- *Jewish.* You've probably already decided to stand under a chuppah (and, yes, couples do include both chuppahs and altars in their weddings) and include a ketubah. Another great idea: personalized yarmulkes with your names and the date of your wedding inscribed inside.
- *Mexican.* A south-of-the-border theme means you've got the whole enchilada to choose from. There's mariachi music, margaritas, a piñata if you're inviting children—or even if you're not—and, of course, a Mexican menu, from tacos to tamales. You should probably include a few milder dishes for the not-so-trained palates among you.
- *Greek.* If you've got a feta fetish, cheese is your answer. For a morning affair, serve it in omelets. Later in the day, add it to salads. Ouzo makes a great drink, and you can always serve baklava for dessert. If you're one of the three people on the planet who've yet to see *My Big Fat Greek Wedding,* rent it now for more ideas.
- *Jamaican.* You'd be a jerk not to include that signature dish—chicken or pork. Rum is the drink of choice, and you should start auditioning those reggae bands now. If you really want to mix it up, mon, make some toasts in patois, the local dialect that combines several languages into one beautiful linguistic tongue-teaser.
- *African American.* Many couples jump the broom, a wedding ritual started by slaves who were not allowed to marry (the broom itself symbolized housekeeping). Red, black, and green color themes are also popular. Variously colored ribbons, headdresses, and variations on some native drumming have also made appearances at these weddings. Also, try out a new hairstyle: Braids make a fine addition for the big day.
- *Spanish.* Paella and sangria complement each other almost as well as the two of you. Orange blossoms, which signify chastity—no, not that Chastity!—are traditionally placed in the bride's bouquet. You might even place them in your hair or incorporate them into centerpieces.

- *Chinese.* Think red. Traditionally, Chinese brides don't wear white. Red gowns or suits would be stunning, as would adding a red boutonniere to any or all outfits. Another custom is to have a large feast—twelve courses is not uncommon—so use your good fortune to have a big meal (shark fin soup is a popular choice).

- *Japanese.* Sushi station, anyone? Also, kimonos would look great on attendants. Karaoke is big in the Land of the Rising Sun, and since the words to the music are always posted for you, your song will never get lost in translation.

- *Filipino.* The Money Dance is common at Philippine weddings. (Either one or both of you take money that is pinned onto your outfit in exchange for a dance.) Also popular is to forgo the bouquet toss and offer the flowers (in a Catholic service) to a favorite saint, or to leave them at the grave site of a loved one.
- *Pakistani.* Terrified of tattoos? Mehndi is the ceremony performed the day before the wedding where the wedding party decorates the bride's and groom's hands with beautiful henna designs. It's a terrific way to honor your heritage. The preparations for these weddings can begin months before the wedding day, and the actual ceremonies can last three days.
- *Hindu.* Make it a sari, sari night for two Indian brides. Traditionally, a priest reads Sanskrit to the new couple—if you're unable to find someone to perform this task, ask a friend to do the honors. After the vows, couples toss rice over each *other's* heads. That should whet your appetite for a wonderful (and very affordable) South Asian feast.
- *Scottish.* While bagpipes play, your guests can try to answer that gay-old question: What does come between a man and his kilt? A popular custom is for the groom to pin a tartan ribbon from his clan onto the bride's dress. Whatever your gender, you can update that tradition by adding a tartan pattern to your outfits.

For more cultural ideas to fit your particular background, try UptownCity .com, weddingthemes.com, or weddinggazette.com, all of which have a fairly comprehensive list of different wedding customs around the world.

Eight

SEX-RATED

Grant & Larry

WHO: Grant Schneider, forty-four, and Larry Diamond, thirty-eight.

WHEN: Friday, September 20, 2002.

WHERE: An eleven A.M. ceremony for forty people on their penthouse terrace, followed by a lunch reception for eighty at New York City's Le Perigord restaurant. Guests were treated to a three-course meal, with dessert and wedding cake.

THE WAY THEY WORE: They each bought suits for the occasion—"more formal than what we'd wear for business," says Larry.

YOU SHOULDN'T BE DANCING: The couple opted for a Brazilian quartet, and no dance floor. "You don't want to make straight people dance," says Grant. Eighty percent of their guests were straight.

DO THESE COME WITH BREAKFAST? The couple registered at Tiffany.

OR HOW ABOUT A RECEIPT? They received twenty crystal tumblers.

TRADITIONAL TOUCHES: A receiving line, two best men, even a same-sex ketubah.

AN OLD-FASHIONED LOVE AFFAIR: Grant made a formal, and unexpected, proposal to Larry. The two men were not living together at the time.

GUYS JUST WANNA HAVE FUN: Both men had bachelor parties; Larry even got sexy underwear from his girlfriends.

WHAT THEY OVERCAME: Figuring out the wedding invitations. They finally decided on "We're Getting Married" as the opener.

PARTY ON: A relative threw them an engagement party in Florida. They had a rehearsal dinner, and ended with a Saturday brunch before jetting off to their honeymoon.

HONEYMOON G-SPOT: First Italy, then Spain (a hotel in Spain gave them the honeymoon suite).

PARTING WORDS: "Our wedding gave us family recognition," says Grant. "That's the case with any marriage. You fall apart when there's no support."

"Sex is best when it's one on one."

—George Michael, "I Want Your Sex"

ou couldn't find a better statement to endorse monogamy. And like the man who said it, you couldn't find one more riddled with irony. When the guy who woke us up before he went-went sang his butt off about the joys of solo sex, he was straight, *fag* meant "feminine," and the only Bush discussed in public was the one about to enter the White House. After a Wham-bam-thank-you-man in a public bathroom, George came out, TV's *Will* turned into amazing grace, and gay life would forever be more than just a stylish alternative.

Now that you're entering into a state of holy matrimony, legally recognized or not, you're going to face challenges your forebearing Stonewallers could only dream about, one of which puts you right next to your heterosexual friends. Yep, you get to face the age-old question that has confounded newlyweds since the dawn of daytime talk shows. Namely, how on earth do you keep the romance alive? Whether you've had years of practice or have only just begun, here's a little sex ed to add to your wedding package. Because sometimes you gotta have more than just faith.

The Mating Game:
Newlywed Dilemmas and How to Deal

Need a little sexual healing? Peruse these problems to help find the answers you need.

THE EX-FILES

You've returned from the honeymoon and settled into your happy new home. At three in the morning, your partner's ex-girlfriend calls to "talk." You:

a. Roll over and go to bed—they've still got issues that need to be worked out.
b. Grab the phone and bawl out the ex. No one's going to mess with your mate.
c. Call an ex-girlfriend of your own. Two can play at this game.

Dealing with exes can be pretty tricky. We all suffer bouts of jealousy, even in the most committed relationships. If your partner refuses to let go of a former lover, or won't admit there's still too much attention being lavished upon her (a 3 A.M. phone call would only be appropriate in the case of an extreme and real emergency), then the two of you need to have a heart-to-heart. If you can't come to some sort of compromise—for example, you could suggest that the ex only communicate with your spouse when the three of you are together—then you might want to get some professional help to resolve the matter. Don't despair, however. A simple pep talk from you may be all she needs to let go of the excess baggage.

Chances are, if you were a heterosexual couple, Mom would be much more inclined to allow the two of you to sleep together. The reality, however, is that not all parents are comfortable with homosexuality—and despite your wedding, they may not approve of cohabitation, at least in their home. The first thing you need to do is let your husband do the talking—he needs to confront his parents about the issue, so that, with any luck, by next year's holiday you can snuggle up together. If his parents are insistent about the sleeping quarters, remember that it *is* their house and you need to respect their wishes. If this is the case, and you cannot fathom the idea of not sleeping together, do call a hotel the next time a holiday reunion rolls around. Or better yet, start a family tradition at *your* new home as a couple.

At some point in your new life together, one or both of you are going to be so overloaded with work that sex will be the last thing on your minds. That's a natural part of the give-and-take of marriage, where compromise is king (or queen). Make sure your wife understands the situation—she might be so busy that she doesn't even realize you're unhappy. If, indeed, your love life suffers for an indefinite period, you don't need to give her an ultimatum, but you can make a deal. Pencil in one night a week when she has to come home early, or schedule a lunchtime rendezvous. Love in the afternoon can be a wonderful thing. And remember, communication is key. So talk about it.

FLIRTING WITH DISASTER

On your tropical-island honeymoon, you notice that the hunky cabana boy winks at your husband. Hubby smiles back and gives him an unusually large tip. You:

a. Call security and have the employee fired. You'll deal with your husband later.
b. Find an even hunkier cabana boy and ask if he does deep-tissue massage—that'll teach your guy.
c. Book the next flight home. There aren't that many hot guys back in Bakersfield.

Let's face it, most of us like to flirt, and it usually amounts to nothing. You and your partner are together because you love each other and are committed to a monogamous relationship. If you do have a spouse who's overt in his attention to others—especially if it means the person on the receiving end might get the wrong impression—talk it out and tell him he needs to limit his flirting to your grandmother and those celluloid jailboys on *Oz*. If your husband had a real desire to meet other men, not even Bakersfield would pose a problem. It is, after all, a matter of trust.

THE COUCH TRIP

You've opened all your wedding gifts and gotten everything you registered for. Unfortunately, your wife seems to take more interest in your new wide-screen TV than in you. The romance must be over. You:

a. Disconnect the cable and cut her Blockbuster card in half. She can stare at *you* for a change.
b. Join her. Who needs real sex when you've got *The L Word*.
c. Put the fish tank where the TV was and perform a striptease behind it. By the time she realizes it's you, the *Finding Nemo* DVD will be lost forever.

There's a myth going around that married life automatically means less sex. Certainly, with all your new adjustments—home, in-laws, children—sex can take a backseat. The truth of the matter, however, is that your wife is probably so enamored of your new life together, she's enjoying all that domestic routines allow, part of which is simply the nearness of you. Take a cue from the second example above and cuddle up to her on the couch. You might be surprised how fast she gets turned on and the TV turned off.

FAT CHANCE

Back when you were engaged, your guy pumped and pressed and lunged till Tuesday. And after sex he went to the gym. Now that you're hitched, he never wants to work out and always finds an excuse to keep him from the health club. You don't need an Adonis for a husband, but you're worried he's going to become one of those beer-bellied guys who thinks good grooming stops after dating. You:

a. Stock the fridge with his favorite ale. If your husband won't maintain his six-pack, he might as well drink one.
b. Stock up on free weights and a StairMaster. If he sees you sweat, it'll motivate him to get back on his routine.
c. Stock up on Snickers bars. You might as well grow old and pudgy together.

"The truth is, like your new marriage, great sex is something you have to work at."

Our society does tend to lend itself to the idea that, once married, you can develop those love handles and let your appearance fall by the wayside. There's also a general consensus that such developments are unavoidable and best transformed into fodder about married life (think of expressions like *my old lady, the old ball and chain,* and Norm's nonstop unromantic jokes about wife Vera on *Cheers*). While weight gain is a natural part of the aging process, and dating involves more maintenance than you'd probably like, being in good health is not only attractive in a relationship, it's also, well, healthy. Both of you can probably afford to loosen up your belts a bit, but try to keep up some kind of sensible health regimen. You'll not only look and feel better, but you'll also have more energy when it's time for the jeans to come off altogether.

THE BETTER SEX

It was a night of wild passion, full of grunts and groans and every fantasy fulfilled. And now that your wife's satisfied, you'd like a little attention yourself. She's become selfish in bed, and the problem's only getting worse. You:

    a. Look in the bathroom mirror and cry. Clearly, she's lost interest in you.

    b. Withhold sex until she learns her lesson. She'll be on you like butter on toast.

    c. Scream and yell till you lose your voice; everyone knows temper tantrums are the solution to every problem.

If only sexual satisfaction were as simple as all those Hollywood love stories led you to believe. The truth is, like your new marriage, great sex is something you have to work at. There's a very good chance that your partner has no idea you're not satisfied. In fact, she might even think she's giving you exactly what you want. Talk it through. Tell her what you'd like, and ask her what she'd like in return—and don't wait until you're in the heat of passion to have this discussion. You both might learn a few new tricks about the communication process, which, of course, means only treats in the bedroom.

OF HUMAN BONDAGE

Ever since the wedding, your love life's been swell. The two of you never grow tired of each other and, no matter what your schedules, you always find time to hit the sheets. Then, one night, your husband brings home sex toys, rope, and a porn video. He says he wants to "experiment." You:

a. Ask if you'll understand the plot of *Bend Over Like Beckham Part 2,* even though you missed the first one.

b. Make sure he knows where the keys are before he cuffs you. You'd hate to have to explain that one to the locksmith.

c. Buy him a chemistry set and tell him he can "experiment" with that!

Sexual experimentation of any kind is entirely up to you and your comfort zone. If your partner wants to play, it doesn't necessarily mean he is tired of you or that outside stimulus is a necessary component of your love life. He may very well think you have the most fabulous sex on earth, and has decided that, with a few props, it can be even more amazing. There is a problem if you're dead set against the idea and he's insistent (in which case you might need to get outside help). Give his suggestions some thought and then be completely honest about what you will or will not do. There's never a time when it's okay for sex to make you uncomfortable. Whatever you decide will absolutely and under every circumstance be the correct answer.

Preventive Medicine

Clearly, the answer in each of the above scenarios is neither a, b, nor c. You *can* help stop any of these situations from ever becoming a reality. While planning your wedding, make sure you take time away from the daily grind to concentrate on your partner's needs. True, it's important that you focus on your own well-being to keep a clear head—whether through exercise, reading, or your favorite CD. But every now and then take stock of what your partner's going through, and why you love this person so much that you've decided to spend the rest of your life by his or her side. Then buy those flowers, make those dinner reservations, or simply turn off the bedroom lights so the world beyond your windows disappears for the night. There's no better prescription for keeping love alive.

ONE-NIGHT STAND: SIZZLING WEDDING-NIGHT TIPS

- *Bar tabs.* Back off on the bubbly. You've had an exciting day full of champagne toasts and winning wines. Too much of the good stuff, however, and come bedtime you'll be too pooped to pop. Keep drinking to a minimum; you want to remember every moment of the day's climactic ending.

- *Underachiever.* At some point near the end of the reception, notify your spouse that you're going to change out of your wedding clothes and into everything but your underwear. Those last remaining guests will be kicked out faster than Tiger Woods at a miniature golf tournament.

- *Over under.* Not the commando type? When you're alone together, make a quick change into something your partner's never seen you wear before. The only rule: It has to be skimpy, purchased somewhere you wouldn't allow your children to enter, and very, very easy to remove.

- *Get a room.* If you're not honeymooning immediately, or at all, make sure you've got a special place to "make it official." Book a hotel room for the night, rather than going home. If you had an at-home wedding, all the more reason to enjoy what room service has to offer.

- *Do not disturb.* On your wedding day, you celebrate in front of your nearest and dearest. On your wedding night, you celebrate alone. Decide upon a reasonable time to make your guests leave the "after party," wherever that may be, and stick to the schedule. Your friends will understand—they'll see that look of love in your eyes.

- *Give it a rest.* What's more important than keeping it hot? *Not* letting it bother you if the first night doesn't end with a bang. While the ideal wedding night equals passion-palooza, you may discover that, after all the celebrating and meeting and greeting, after tears and vows and reunions with loved ones, you'd simply like to end the evening on a quiet note, reflecting on your good fortune with the one you love. And there's nothing wrong with that.

HEAVENLY HONEYMOONS

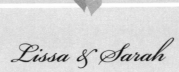

Lissa & Sarah

WHO: Lissa, twenty-six, and Sarah, twenty-seven, Mantell.

WHEN: Saturday, October 27, 2003.

WHERE: The Hyatt Regency, Bethesda, Maryland. Eighty guests for a nighttime ceremony. The guests were treated to a cocktail hour, and a four-course, seated meal of American cuisine customized by the two brides.

YOU GOTTA HAVE FRIENDS: "The banquet manager became a really good friend," says Lissa. "He's gay, and he probably threw himself into the project more than he normally would have."

. . . AND MORE FRIENDS: "We knew the Hyatt was the perfect place," Lissa adds. "As soon as I called them and told them it was a commitment ceremony, the woman congratulated us. From that point on, every manager involved made a point of coming over to meet us and wish us well."

TRADITIONAL TOUCHES: Both brides wore ivory wedding dresses; each had attendants and bouquets. There was a father—daughter dance, a cake cutting, a rehearsal dinner of bar food—"a great way for our guests to all meet each other before the ceremony," says Lissa—and a joint bachelorette party.

WHY IT WAS WISE THEY DIDN'T PARTY THE NIGHT BEFORE: "We bar-hopped and got free shots wherever we went," says Sarah. "I couldn't move the next day."

KEEPING THEIR RELIGION: A lesbian rabbi officiated. During the wine blessing, she spilled drops on the saucer to symbolize that gay equality in marriage has not yet been achieved.

WALK THIS WAY: The brides walked each other down the aisle. Says Sarah: "We've been together six years. We weren't going to let someone else give us away."

QUEER NATION: "When we went to Crate & Barrel to register, there were at least half a dozen other gay couples there," Lissa says.

WHAT THEY OVERCAME: The couple had planned on cookie-cutter favors—Sarah's a pastry chef. Right before the wedding, the company they'd ordered them from failed to deliver. In a panic, Lissa went to the same-sex bridal chat room on theknot.com and asked for help. "A woman told us she had a hundred left over from her own wedding, and insisted on FedExing them the next day. She wouldn't even let me pay her. It was wonderful and a great omen."

HONEYMOON G-SPOT: A week in Palm Springs.

PARTING WORDS: Says Sarah: "It was wonderful to dance and celebrate with all our friends and loved ones. We decided, Why wait till it's legal? If the world catches up with us, great!"

*A*lthough you should start planning your honeymoon five to seven months before the wedding, we put this chapter in last because it's the final step of your new beginning. You're about to embark on a magnificent journey, and, no matter where you end up, your hearts will always find a home. When the guests have left and the music stops, when the laughter fades and the tears go dry, it's just the two of you, alone, together, and in love.

Have a wonderful trip!

Choices, Choices

Did you ever think the word *honeymoon* would apply to you? Not so long ago, when gay couples wed, they spent their alone time afterward at a friend's beach cottage in Provincetown, at a bed-and-breakfast in San Francisco, or, quite possibly, holed up alone in their Greenwich Village walk-up. While all of the above options can make for a fantastic postwedding celebration, there's a whole new world of honeymoon options out there, one of which should be just right for the two of you.

Whether you want to be surrounded by "family" or lost in a sea of mainstream love, go global or stay close to home, here's how to pick a place, plan your time, and lose yourself under the thoughtful gaze of the *person* in the moon.

Arriving in Style

Here's a little-known fact you won't find out from reading *Straight Travel Weekly*: The tourism industry wants you! Destinations are catching on that homosexuals like to travel just like everyone else and, more important, gay couples tend to have more disposable income than a lot of heterosexuals with large families. What this means for you is that more and more destinations are reaching out to a gay audience. In other words, unless a resort is run by incredibly bigoted, or not particularly business-savvy, management (in either case, these are places you'd rather avoid), you're more than likely to find yourself welcomed with open arms. After all, you're the ones opening the purse strings.

When planning your trip, you have the option of going through a travel agent (contact the American Society of Travel Agents at 703-739-2782 or www.astanet.com, and tell them you need to speak with someone who specializes in honeymoons), or going it alone with guidebooks, the Internet, and, of course, references from friends. The advantage of travel agents is that they may know of even better deals than you'll find on the Web, and they can help you customize your honeymoon—plus, you'll get the kind of personal service that a good Google just can't match. The disadvantage could be the very same thing: Some people would rather not have a stranger arranging their honeymoon. Also, a travel agent might be unaware that finding a hotel near a Hard Rock Café is not a priority.

Whichever route you choose, make sure the hotel you're staying at is informed that you're on your honeymoon. Just as with straight couples—it's uncanny how similar we all are!—there's a chance you'll get an upgrade, a bottle of bubbly or box of chocolates, or something perhaps even more important—privacy. Also, should your travels take you to the Caribbean or any seaside spot, be sure to ask for a room with an ocean view. Taking in that deep blue water as you take in your honey's baby blues is always worth the price of admission. Should you find that you get stuck with a room overlooking the parking lot, call the front desk and ask for a better one. Hotels make mistakes, too. It may simply have been a booking oversight.

Remember, resorts depend on repeat visitors. Honeymooners, if satisfied with their vacation spot, are extremely likely to return on anniversaries, birthdays, or at any other time they can get away again to relive those wonderful days and nights. In this day and age, that means you, too.

Prep Work

No matter where you go, you want to make sure you've covered all the essentials that traveling requires. This could mean anything from packing toothpaste to getting malaria shots. To help simplify your planning, here are some basic preparation essentials:

- *Papers, please.* If you're going abroad, make sure your passports are current. Some countries may require a visa: Check with the tourism bureau of your chosen destination. Before you leave, make photocopies of all documents, including your credit cards, and leave them with friends in case of an emergency. If either one of you is changing your name, make sure you make all reservations in the legal moniker that appears on the identification you'll be taking on the trip. You've got years to be Mr. and Mr. Roger Romance; there's no reason to confuse the customs people now.
- *Give me a shot.* Find out what, if any, immunizations you need in preparation for your trip, and arrange for them immediately. Contact the Centers for Disease Control (cdc.gov), which has an extensive list of what vaccines and immunizations are required or requested around the world, as well as the latest news on any potential health threats in the area. If you don't already know not to drink the tap water in Mexico, this website will handily remind you.
- *Suspended in time.* Call and arrange to have your newspaper held, or

arrange for a friend to pick it up. If you live in an apartment that employs a doorman, they will usually hold the paper for you. For security purposes, it's also a good idea to keep a car parked in the driveway, keep some lights on, and have a trusted neighbor swing by while you're away to check up on things. Also, leave contact information—and a copy of your itinerary—in case of emergency. And bring these friends back a great gift for all their help!

- *Package deal.* We know you're busy, but don't put off packing until the last minute: It's a surefire way to forget that fabulous bathing suit you've been waiting months to show off. A few reminders: Carry any essentials (medications, a change of clothing, cell phone, arrival contacts) in your carry-on. This way, should your luggage be lost, you won't end up stranded in Singapore, with your essentials in Tokyo. It's also a great idea to carry the name and number of your doctors back home in case one of you gets sick.

- *Excess baggage.* General rule of thumb: When in doubt, don't pack it! Sure, it would be nice to have three separate outfits for each day, but if you're going to be lugging this stuff around a lot, prioritize and pack light. Go through your suitcase and take out the seven extra sweaters you thought would look dazzling in Denmark. Keep in mind, too, that a lot of people like to shop on their honeymoon. If this sounds like you, you'll need room in your suitcase to bring home the goods—including those Bulgari bathroom products you "accidentally" remove from your suite.

- *Personal shopper.* It's not very difficult to locate sunscreen in the Bahamas. What might be troublesome is finding it for a decent rate. Chances are most resorts will have what you need (mosquito repellent, film, even condoms)—but at a cost that will make you think you've miscalculated the exchange rate. Before you go, make a list and head to the corner drugstore for these international traveling basics. You'll save money, and it will be one less thing to worry about once you reach paradise.

- *Expense report.* Gone are the days when traveling meant you had to turn all your bills into traveler's checks. You can certainly still use them (in general, hotels and restaurants will cash them, though you might have more difficulty at a Jamaican jerk joint). Now, with ATMs just about everywhere, the money situation has become a machine-made dream. Do, however, check ahead to make sure your chosen honeymoon heaven has them (you're not going to encounter a problem in Italy, but some destinations in the Caribbean have only a few ATMs—and, in our experience, they often don't work). Get a small amount of the local currency before you leave. Remember, too, that if you get stuck, you can ask your hotel about a credit card cash advance. Finally, save a few small bills for immediate tipping needs. Taxi drivers and bellboys are your friends—offering up an IOU is a sure way to lose an important (where's the nearest bathroom, quick?) alliance. The concierge not only is your friend, but can also be your social coordinator. Slip him some bills before you ask him about local entertainment, how to get that corner table at tonight's booked-up restaurant, and, perhaps most important, where *is* the best gay bar in town?

- *Another budget buster.* They may call them minibars, but they come at a maximum price. Unless you're keen on paying four bucks for a bag of peanuts, try to find a local convenience store and stock up. If the temptation for treats is too much, ask at check-in if they'll keep the bar door locked or unstocked. Room service is also outrageously expensive, but if you're going to splurge, this is where to do it. A resort rule that we've made over the years: If the room service coffee tastes great and is presented well (complimentary muffins, linen napkins), then the rest of the in-room dining is probably worth it. If a five-star hotel can't make a decent pot of coffee, then forget ordering chocolate cake when you've got the midnight munchies. Your wallet and your waistline will both resent it.

We're Here, We're Queer, Where Do We Go from Here?

Once you've settled in to your dream cottage, beach shack, or hip high-rise, there are a few things to keep in mind:

- If you plan on bringing a personal computer to a destination outside the United States, check to see if you'll need an electrical converter to accommodate the electrical voltage in different countries. (Guidebooks will usually provide this information.) In the end, you might decide carrying your computer isn't worth the potential hassles; besides, you've got plenty of other ways to utilize your lap.

- As for those wireless minutes, this is the time to use them up. Hotel phone charges are outrageously expensive. Check with your cell phone service provider to see if your phone is operable at your honeymoon location. Most providers will let you change your service options for a limited number of days and, if you do this while traveling, the money you'll save by not using the hotel phones will definitely be worth it.

- Always bring at least one guidebook on your trip, even if you never intend to leave the hotel room. You'll find vital information about emergency services, including embassy contacts should you get into legal trouble, and where to go if you or your spouse has a medical problem. Any reputable guidebook, such as Frommer's or Fodor's, will have information on gay travel and any safety tips of which you should be aware. If you're concerned with gay-friendliness, check to see if your destination is a member of the International Gay and Lesbian Travel Association (www.IGLTA.com), alternative travel associations that can tell you if your hotel makes the "gay okay" list. Also visit gaydestination.com for spots that welcome folk as queer as you.

- Since tipping amounts vary depending on your destination, do some research before you go, and ask what the policies are both in different countries and at your specific hotel or resort. For instance, rumor has it that in Germany people get offended if you overtip (we know someone, however, who dropped a lot of cash at the Four Seasons bar in Munich, and got both a free drink and a big smile from the bartender). Many tipping rules vary depending on how "American" the resort is—meaning, if they're used to U.S. guests, they're probably used to U.S. tips. Make sure to read the bill carefully, because gratuities are often included.

- Another tip tip: Don't wait till the end of your stay to pay the maids. Put down some bills each day—you might find a few extra mints on your even-fluffier pillows.

Do You Know Where You're Going To?

Where you end up depends on your budget, how much time you have, and what your interests are. If one of you loves to ski and the other's a beach buff, go where the season takes you and save the alternative for a change in the weather. One of the biggest quandaries for homosexual honeymooners is whether they should go gay (Hello, Fort Lauderdale!) or straight (Aloha!). Lucky for you, the choice is no longer so black and white. While specifically gay destinations abound, many "straight" traditional honeymoon spots are surprisingly gay-friendly. Hawaii, for instance, is increasingly attracting more same-sex visitors for both weddings and honeymoons (visit konaweddings.com for information on the fiftieth state). And as any frequent gay traveler, or travel writer, can tell you, there's nary a prime vacation or honeymoon spot these days that doesn't host some sort of local gay community. In notoriously homophobic Jamaica, for example, same-sex couples are now welcomed at some of the island's best resorts. Be sure to look up Mockingbird Hill in Port Antonio and Round Hill in Montego Bay. Take a stroll down the side streets of Mexico's Playa del Carmen, and you'll see enough men kissing that you just might think you've stepped into Miami Beach.

Here are some famous honeymoon spots that have opened their doors to happy homosexual campers:

- *Niagara Falls.* It's not just your parents' destination anymore. The Ramada Inn by the Falls welcomes same-sex couples who want to fall all over again: 716-282-1734 or ramada.com. On the Canadian side is exclusively gay Oasis Niagara Bed and Breakfast: 905-353-0223 or oasisniagara.com.
- *Lake Tahoe.* Check out romanticgayweddings.com for same-sex sites at this year-round California/Nevada treasure.
- *Atlantic City.* The Surfside Resort Hotel means same-sex honeymooning here is no longer a gamble. Contact 888-277-SURF or surfsideresorthotel.com.
- *Walt Disney World and Disneyland.* It truly is a magic kingdom once a year, when Gay Days lures thousands of gays and lesbians to the parks to wish

upon their stars. Disney, in general, has a great reputation with the gay community. If you and your partner ask for the honeymoon package any time of year, they'll welcome you with open ears. Visit gaydays.com and gayday2.com for information.

- *Maui.* Gays can get lei'd (and have a wedding!) on this tropical beauty. Contact gaymauiwedding.com.
- *Palm Springs.* Former party place of the Rat Pack and the Frat Packs, this desert oasis is now decidedly gay. Contact gay-palm-springs.info for honeymoon hot spots.
- *The* Queen Mary 2. With a name like that, it's only fitting that the Cunard Line's newest ocean liner would be gay-accommodating. Keep in mind that you'll need cocktail dresses, cuff links, and plenty of cash. Contact Cunard.com to get in ship shape.
- *The Poconos.* Home of champagne-glass-shaped Jacuzzis, heart-shaped beds, and now homos, this Pennsylvania resort area boasts several same-sex-welcomed resorts. There's even a gay disco. Go to rainbowmountain .com, then turn on the jets.
- *Europe.* Gays will always have Paris . . . and Switzerland, and Spain. Europe, in general, is far more relaxed about homosexuality than other parts of the world, so don't fret if you want to take in Big Ben on your honeymoon. For good guidance, we recommend *Frommer's Gay and Lesbian Europe,* available wherever books are sold.
- *Washington, D.C.* Okay, so it's not typically associated with honeymoon travel. But with so many gay neighborhoods flanking the White House, D.C. is worth considering. Cruise through the Smithsonian by day then, come nightfall, watch the cruising at JRs, a bar where everybody who's ever known anybody who's gay eventually shows up. Extra points if you spot a senator. Go to mygayworld.com for capital ideas.
- *The Caribbean.* If you thought the Caribbean was only all-*exclusive* resorts like Sandals, think again. You can be like a virgin on the USVI, play like a princess in Puerto Rico, shed your clothing on Saba and St. Maarten, and go gay Dutch on Curaçao. For a comprehensive list of gay-friendly accommodations on the turquoise sea, go to gaytravel.com and click on "Caribbean."

You Can Go Your Own Gay Way

If you'd like to be sure that your honeymoon is exclusively female, exclusively male, or gay-only, consider these options: Board an all-gay cruise (some are just for the ladies); show off your inner jock at a Club Med gay week; or do it Down Under—Melbourne and Sydney both have highly visible gay populations, the latter city hosting an annual gay and lesbian Mardis Gras (womenstravelinternational.com is a great site if you want to travel to Australia with just the gals). Back in the USA, southern comfort never felt so good as in Savannah, where gay-owned and -friendly resorts are popping up with charm aplenty. It's big *and* easy to be a same-sex couple in New Orleans, with dozens of rainbow-bedecked hotels and B&Bs to choose from. Now that Massachusetts has become the center of gay politics, beachside Province-town's summer rentals are filling up year-round. While everyone knows you can leave your heart in San Francisco, travel an hour and a half northwest and you'll hit the Russian River, with forest trails (think of it as Fire Island with logs), wine tastings nearby, and a gay glasnost stretch of water. Birthplace of the first U.S. civil unions, Vermont will gladly host your postwedding bliss; New York's Chelsea is where the boys go; and homosexuals of both sexes are setting up camp, literally, all across the United States.

Here are some resources that will get you started on your globe-trotting adventures. Let your imagination be your guide—and see Resources in the back of this book for even more suggestions.

www.atlantisevents.com
www.gaydestination.com
www.gayfriendlyinns.com
www.gayguide.net
www.gaytravel.com
www.lambdaresorts.com
www.olivia.com
www.outtraveler.com (*The Out Traveler*)
www.passportmagazine.com (*Passport Magazine*)
www.purpleroofs.com

www.sistertrip.com

www.womenstravelinternational.com

You've Only Just Begun

Where does the time go? Here you are planning a honeymoon when it seems like only yesterday that you decided to wed. Since the moment you said "we will," you've signed contracts, picked color palettes, and dealt with more drama than a daytime soap. (Worried you've missed something? We've got a complete Wedding Countdown Calendar next, to make sure you keep in step.) Though you've probably had a few tiffs in the process, we hope you've managed to keep your sense of humor and, more important, we hope you've had fun. Because even if the flowers arrived on time—but at the wrong location—or your pet pooch never quite made his mark—except the one on your dress—at the end of your day those are mere trifles. The only thing that really matters is what comes next, as you assume your new roles as partners for life. If you think you've learned something about weddings from reading this book, just think what the rest of the world is learning from knowing about you. Love isn't determined by gender or law, and commitment doesn't come from a piece of paper. Your decision to stand in front of the world and say your vows stems from a force unbreakable by conventional rules. In your case, getting married and having a wedding is a decision purely from the heart.

This is one of the most important, hopeful, and loving times of your lives. We're thrilled we could help out along the way.

Wedding Countdown Calendar

12 MONTHS

_____ Purchase wedding planner.

_____ Determine budget. (Guys, now double it—you'll thank us later. Gals, you can probably afford to spend a bit more.)

_____ Think about style of wedding, including size, place, and attendants (if any).

_____ Set the date.

_____ Mail save-the-date cards, if you're having a long-distance wedding or are marrying over a holiday weekend.

_____ Book ceremony and reception sites.

_____ Make a wish list of wedding must-haves. Popular vendors book early; call now if you've got your heart set on that fabulous florist or cool rock band.

Join a gym! (For those of you in living in Chelsea, Miami, or Los Angeles, just make sure your membership's current; and if you're not into contact sports, sign up for some yoga.)

11 MONTHS

_____ If you've put off anything from the above, do it now! This is the only warning you will receive.

_____ Decide if you'll be incorporating religion into your service. If yes, find out if your house of worship offers alternative ceremonies. If not, start looking elsewhere.

_____ Read up on current same-sex-union laws in your state, and get paperwork started if you plan to legalize your relationship.

10 MONTHS

_____ Decide what traditional (hetero) wedding customs you'd like to include or exclude—cake, traditional vows, first dances, etc. If you're wearing a bridal gown, start shopping now.

_____ Compile a list of vendors—caterers, florists, photographers—compare prices, and narrow down your search.

_____ Make sure everyone coming knows you're gay. ("I'm too involved with my work to get involved" is getting old, and so is "Until men mature I'd simply rather hang out with my girlfriend.")

HEAVENLY
HONEYMOONS

9 MONTHS

_____ Make time for friends you've been neglecting. Remember, they have lives, too.

_____ Make a fitness goal so that you look and feel great on the big day—something more than reading the *Men's Health* and *Glamour* headlines.

8 MONTHS

_____ Book all vendors.

_____ Register for gifts.

_____ Make up a preliminary guest list.

_____ Order a wedding dress, if you're going traditional.

7 MONTHS

_____ Decide what type of honeymoon you want and research destinations. If you book early, you'll save money.

_____ Rent any supplies you'll need for the wedding—chairs, tent, tables, etc.

_____ Book hotel rooms for out-of-town guests (ask about discounts for large groups). If you live in a small city, you can probably do this during month six.

_____ Shop for bridesmaids' dresses, if applicable.

6 MONTHS

_____ Order all stationery, including thank-you notes.

_____ Go over the music list with your DJ and/or band.

_____ Choose a menu with your caterer.

_____ Make a final decision on all flowers.

5 MONTHS

_____ If you haven't yet, book your honeymoon.

_____ Renew or apply for passports, if necessary.

_____ Determine and reserve all transportation.

_____ Check and update your wedding registry. (If no one's bought that Hermès dog collar or the Crate & Barrel hibachi grill yet, start dropping hints.)

4 MONTHS

_____ Select all traditionally male formalwear—suits and tuxedos.

_____ Order your rings.

_____ Finalize your guest list.

_____ Let friends know if you'd like to have bachelor/bachelorette parties, so they can start planning and figure out the best time.

_____ Have your portrait taken to send to the newspaper, if applicable.

3 MONTHS

_____ Make decisions on ceremony specifics. If you'd like friends or relatives to speak, recite a poem, etc., ask them now.

_____ Decide who's walking you down the aisle.

_____ Still haven't lost the weight? Cut out the ice cream and switch to fat-free desserts (for those of you living in Chelsea, Miami, or Los Angeles, fire your trainer: He's clearly not doing his job).

2 MONTHS

_____ Mail invitations.

_____ Write vows.

_____ Buy gifts for each other, attendants, and parents.

_____ Men, if your're taking his name, notify all relative parties. Buy smelling salts before telling Mom. Women, if you're changing your name, notify all relative parties. If she's taking your name, tell Dad it's kind of like preserving the family line.

1 MONTH

_____ Sort RSVPs as they come in and begin making the final guest list.

_____ Update your registry if necessary.

_____ Send out thank-you cards to anyone who's sent you presents in lieu of attending the wedding.

3 WEEKS

_____ Check with any invitee who hasn't gotten back to you. If necessary, invite other guests.

_____ Head out for drinks with your buds. Don't discuss the wedding, the honeymoon, or whether or not you're butch enough!

2 WEEKS

_____ Finalize the guest list and start writing out table and place cards if you are going to use them. Figure out who will get along with whom and where they should sit. (We recommend buying presentation materials, a laser pen, and extra-strength Tylenol.)

_____ Put passports, travel tickets, and itineraries together in one place. Confirm any flight information and hotel reservations.

_____ Discuss any photographic or musical requirements, including shot and song selections, with your photographer and/or videographer and DJ or band.

_____ Complete any toasts or vow writing that you've yet to do.

1 WEEK

_____ Give all vendors a call to double-check that no one has any questions and everyone knows what day and where your wedding is actually being held.

_____ Make sure that all people playing a role in your reception are aware of what they should be doing (or reading) and when.

_____ Give your final guest number to the caterer.

_____ Pick up your tux or other formalwear. Try it on to make sure there are no problems. Hang it in a garment bag or plastic in a closet where dirty gym clothes are never stored.

Bachelor/ette party? Make sure the stripper isn't an ex.

DAY BEFORE

_____ Hold the rehearsal dinner if you are planning one.

_____ Lay low on the alcohol and go to bed early.

_____ As for the weight you didn't lose? Relax, your partner loves you for who you are.

DAY OF

Have the most wonderful time of your life!

RESOURCES

ADOPTION

"Adoption by Gays and Lesbians: A National Survey of Adoption Agency Policies, Practices and Attitudes," released by the Evan B. Donaldson Adoption Institute on October 29, 2003; adoptioninstitute.org
adoptions.com/gaylez.html

BRIDAL DRESSES

davidsbridal.com
theknot.com
weddingchannel.com

EXPOS/EVENTS

gayweddingshows.com
lagayweddingexpo.com
rainbowweddingnetwork.com

FLOWERS

1800flowers.com

GIFT REGISTRY

Bed Bath & Beyond
    bedbathandbeyond.com
Crate&Barrel
    crateandbarrel.com
Home Depot
    homedepot.com
Macy's
    macys.com
Michael C. Fina
    michaelcfina.com
Rainbow Wedding Network
    rainbowweddingnetwork.com
Tiffany & Co.
    tiffany.com
The Knot
    theknot.com
WeddingChannel
    weddingchannel.com
Your Registry
    Yourweddingregistry.com

GUIDEBOOKS

Frommer's Gay and Lesbian Europe: The Top Cities & Resorts, 3rd edition, by
    David Andrusia, Memphis Barbree, Haas Mrove, and Donald Olson
*Queens in the Kingdom: The Ultimate Gay and Lesbian Guide to the Disney
Theme Parks* by Jeffrey Epstein and Eddie Shapiro

HONEYMOON (TRAVEL WEBSITES AND ORGANIZATIONS)

Access America (travel insurance)
    800-284-8300 or www.accessamerica.com
American Society of Travel Agents
    703-739-2782 or www.astanet.com
atlantisevents.com
Cunard.com
gay.australia.com
gay-australia.net
gayaustraliaguide.bigstep.com
gaydays.com
gayday2.com
gaydestination.com
gayfriendlyinns.com
gayguide.net
gaymauiwedding.com
gay-palm-springs.info
gayneworleans.com
gaysavannah.com
gaytravel.com
gogayaustralia.com
hawaiigayweddings.com
International Gay and Lesbian Travel Association
    www.IGLTA.com
konaweddings.com
lambdaresorts.com
lesbian.com
lesbianadventuretravel.com
mygayworld.com
olivia.com
outandabout.com

outtraveler.com

passportmagazine.com

ptown.org

purpleroofs.com

qtmagazine.com

rainbowglobe.com

rainbowmountain.com

romanticgayweddings.com

sistertrip.com

virginvows.com

womenstravelinternational.com

HOTELS

The following hotels have provided valuable assistance in putting this book together:

Avila Beach Hotel, Curaçao
    800-747-8162 or avilahotel.com
Four Seasons Hotels and Resorts
    fourseasons.com
Hotel Kura Hulanda, Curaçao
    877-264-3106 or kurahulanda.com
Hotel Mockingbird Hill, Jamaica
    876-993-7267 or hotelmockingbirdhill.com
Oasis Niagara Bed and Breakfast:
    905-353-0223 or oasisniagara.com
Ramada Inn by the Falls, Niagara Falls, N.Y.
    716-282-1734 or ramada.com
Round Hill Hotel and Villas Resort, Jamaica
    800-972-2159 or roundhilljamaica.com

Surfside Resort Hotel
888-277-SURF or surfsideresorthotel.com
The Madison Hotel, Washington, D.C.
800-424-8577 or themadisondc.com
Walt Disney Parks and Resorts
disney.com

INFORMATION/MISCELLANEOUS GAY RESOURCES

The Advocate
advocate.com
Gay.com
Gay, Lesbian, Bisexual and Transgender Information
glbtcentral.com
Gay and Lesbian Yellow Pages
glyp.com
Out.com
Planetout.com

INVITATIONS

911weddinginvitations.com
commitment-ceremonies.com
gayweddinginvitations.com
nicolerivera.com
pridebride.com
twogrooms.com
twobrides.com
unionoflove.com
wedding.orders.com
weddingplanningwiz.com/gay
theamericanwedding.com

INVITATION SOFTWARE

ed-it.com
mountaincow.com (PrintingPress Pro software)
weddingsoft.com

PHOTOGRAPHY

Brian Appel Photography
    212-563-5929 or brianappelphotography.com
Freestyle Inc. Photo-Graphic
    888-397-9933 or freestylephoto.com
Piero Ribelli
    212-463-7195 or pieroribelli.com
Sarah Merians Photography
    sarahmerians.com

POLITICS/LEGAL ISSUES

American Civil Liberties Union
    aclu.org
Freedom to Marry
    www.freedomtomarry.org
Gay and Lesbian Advocates and Defenders
    glad.org
Gay and Lesbian Alliance Against Defamation
    glaad.org
Human Rights Campaign
    hrc.org
Human Rights Watch
    hrw.org
Lambda Legal
    Lambdalegal.org

Marriage in Canada
    vs.gov.bc.ca/marriage/howto.html
National Gay and Lesbian Task Force
    thetaskforce.org
theweddingparty.org

RELIGION

christianlesbians.com

*Major World Religions on the Question of Marriage: A Research Summary from
    the Catholic University of America Marriage Law Project*
    marriagelaw.cua.edu/religion.htm
MCC Church
    mcchurch.org
Ontario Consultants on Religious Tolerance
    religioustolerance.org
People for the American Way
    pfaw.org
rainbowchristians.com

RINGS

Jewelers of America
    National Association for Retail Jewelers
    jewelers.org
Jewelry Information Center (JIC)
    jewelryinfo.org

TRANSPORTATION

BLS Limousine Service
    blslimo.com
limo.org

WEDDING PLANNING, GENERAL

brides.com

Confetti Cakes, New York, NY
   212-877-9580 or confetticakes.com

Hand-Sculpted Wedding Cake Toppers
   540-459-7664 or themcdevittstudio.com

Imagine Weddings & Events International
   imaginevip.com (click on "Same Sex Weddings")

junewedding.com

Lotus Flowers, New York, N.Y.
   212-463-0555 or lotus212.com

mariamcbride.com

modernbride.com

WEDDING PLANNING SOFTWARE

fivestarsoftware.com/gaywedding

frogwaresoftware.com

smartwedding.com

theessentialweddingplanner.com

weddingsoft.com

weddingtracker.com

ACKNOWLEDGMENTS

No book is an island, and the following people, places, and organizations have to be thanked for their invaluable contributions to this project:

Shelley Clark and Lou Hammond & Associates, 39 East 51st Street, New York, NY 10022 (212-308-8880 or louhammond.com).

Cathy Renna at Fenton Communications, 260 Fifth Avenue, New York, NY 10001 (212-584-5000 or fenton.com).

The Gay and Lesbian Alliance Against Defamation (GLAAD; www.glaad.org).

Cilantro restaurant, 244 East 79th Street, New York, NY 10021 (212-537-7745 or cilantronyc.com).

Confetti Cakes, 102 West 87th Street, New York, NY 10024 (212-877-9580 or confetticakes.com).

Lotus Flowers, 161 Seventh Avenue, New York, NY 10014 (212-463-0555 or lotus212.com).

Tavern on the Green restaurant, Central Park West at 67th Street, New York, NY 10023 (212-873-4111 or tavernonthegreen.com).

Models: Rose Austin-Ribelli, Danielle Durkin, Andrea Fraccari, Damon Garcia, Jennifer Gerardi, Susanne Gutermuth, Nickey Henry, Laura Hetzel, Dana Isaacson, Eun–Gyu Lee, Adelle McDermott, Ed McKenna, Grant Neumann, Hughes-Bernard Saulnerond, Alex Southgate, Foteini Tsigarida, Christina Gecko Walsh, and Bob Zuckerman.

DAVID TOUSSAINT would like to thank the following: First, to Danielle Durkin and everyone at Ballantine Books for giving me such a wonderful opportunity (and for having the courage and conviction to carry out this venture). Also, to everyone behind the scenes—if I tried to name you all personally, I'd inevitably leave someone out—who has worked above and beyond the call of duty to make sure all of the elements of this book came together so beautifully. To PJ Mark, who's not only a brilliant agent, but whose passion, guidance, and patience in dealing with this writer make me think I'll be punished in my next life by having to represent *him*. To fab photographer Piero Ribelli, who falsely believes his Italian accent is what draws people to him: It's really his personality—now that's amore! To Heather Leo, whose work ethic would make any Protestant blush, and who's so talented that by the time this book comes out she probably won't be taking my calls. To Bill Werde, who knows a good story when it presents itself, and then reports on it with integrity and without compromise. Finally, to my mother, Leona, who every day practices her belief that the human heart is our guiding principle. Thanks, Mom!

HEATHER LEO would like to thank the following: To David Toussaint, for picking me to be on your team while you hammered out witty page after page, night after night. I've learned so much during this adventure; thanks for the opportunity. (P.S. I still think the crime drama photo was the way to go, but that's just me.) To Danielle Durkin and PJ Mark, thanks for being so wonderful to work with. Your intelligence, efficiency, and diligence has been extraordinary (not to mention taxing on my Yahoo! account storage). To the folks at Ballantine Books, thanks for believing in the project and getting it out there. To my parents, who raised me to be independent and confident in my beliefs (even when they might not understand or agree with them); my cousin Nicole, who is all-knowing; my friends, especially Vicky, Ellen, Dana, Carol, Kate, Karen, Tim, Christy, and Geraldine; and mentors, Sally, Barrie, Nancy, Liz, and Irene—thanks for inspiring me, encouraging me, and listening to all of my blah-blah-blah-ing 24/7. I love you all.

DAVID TOUSSAINT is a freelance writer, playwright, actor, and director. He has been a contributing editor and travel writer for Condé Nast Publications, and was a frequent writer for *Bride's* magazine. He has just completed his second play, and is currently at work on a novel. He lives in Manhattan.

HEATHER LEO has written for and was assistant editor of the beauty and jewelry sections at *Bride's* magazine. She is currently the associate beauty editor at *Organic Style* magazine.